A WHO'S WHO OF WORCESTERSHIRE COUNTY CRICKET CLUB

A Who's Who of

Robert
Brooke
and
David
Goodyear

Worcestershire County Cricket Club

ROBERT HALE · LONDON

© *Copyright Robert Brooke and David Goodyear 1990*
First published in Great Britain 1990

Robert Hale Limited
Clerkenwell House
Clerkenwell Green
London EC1R 0HT

British Library Cataloguing in Publication Data

Brooke, Robert

A who's who of Worcestershire Country Cricket Club.
1. Hereford and Worcester. Worcestershire. County cricket.
Clubs. Worcestershire County Cricket Club – Biographies –
Collections
I. Title   II. Goodyear, David
796.35'8'0922

ISBN 0–7090–4023–7

Photoset in Times by
Derek Doyle & Associates, Mold, Clwyd.
Printed in Great Britain by
St Edmundsbury Press, Bury St Edmunds, Suffolk.
Bound by WBC Bookbinders Limited.

Contents

Illustrations

In the process of writing this book, the authors have discovered a number of hitherto unseen portraits of Worcestershire players. The quality of photographs varies considerably, however, according to age and rarity, and it is hoped that readers will appreciate that reproduction has been difficult in some cases.

Half- and full-page illustrations are listed below.

In assembling a book of this nature it is difficult to trace all owners of original illustration material. If we have unintentionally failed to acknowledge any photographer, we would like to apologize and suggest you contact us, care of our publishers.

R.B. & D.G.

Foreword

by Revd Mike Vockins, Secretary of WCCC

For someone whose appreciation of statistics is sketchy and whose knowledge of history is hazy I cannot but admire those who so dedicatedly research our game's history and records.

These enthusiastic students and scholars take great pride in establishing the accuracy of their findings, some of which must take great patience and tenacity to track down. Then, no sooner have they brought all their information together and published it than someone comes along and establishes a new record, makes a bigger score or in some way alters what is known. That must be frustrating; it would certainly frustrate me!

However, such is the love which cricket stimulates in its followers that these researchers gain great pleasure from finding, and then adding, more pieces to cricket's richly painted jigsaw. Without all those pieces, without all the research, without the meticulous tracking-down of information, and without careful recording of detail, cricket's history and tradition would largely be unknown. There would be no base from which we could work, and from which further researches can begin. Our understanding and appreciation of the game would be poorer.

David Goodyear and Robert Brooke have worked with typical enthusiasm and tenacity to bring together the information in this who's who of Worcestershire cricketers. Undoubtedly they will have enjoyed their task, and their enjoyment will be matched by those who read their book and by those who will constantly refer to it.

Preface

The compilation of this second of a projected series of illustrated County Cricket Who's Whos has presented more difficulties than the previous volume on Warwickshire. For various reasons Worcestershire has had a higher number of players, both amateur and professional, who have flitted across the first-class scene and then were heard of no more. Typical of such players was M. Bennett, who played a single game against the Combined Services in 1946. Research in contemporary newspapers has elicited no information on this player – and Roly Jenkins, off whose bowling Bennett took his only catch in first-class cricket, has no memory of him. In this, and a few other cases, we admit defeat, but hope that the publication of this book may well strike a chord in someone's memory, or even bring forward some of the missing players.

Much of the groundwork for the Worcestershire biographies was done several years ago by various members of the Association of Cricket Statisticians, especially Tim Neilson and Philip Thorn, and their work has been continued, supplemented and, where necessary, amended. The club's statistics have lately been in the hands of Les Hatton, who willingly supplied all the limited overs career figures for this work, and while the first-class figures are the work of the authors, they have been much improved through comparison with those of Hatton, which have appeared in various places of late.

Several former players have kindly supplied photographs and information, while we have been grateful for the more general interest shown by Roly Jenkins and Norman Whiting, whose loquacity has been both entertaining and informative. The Worcestershire secretary, Mike Vockins, has given us every support, while as usual with regard to the research involved in such publications, the assistance at various libraries has been greatly appreciated.

D.G. & R.B.

Acknowledgements

Our thanks are due to: N.T. Pearson, L. Bill and G. Harper of Stourbridge CC; Frances Cartwright and staff, *Wolverhampton Express & Star*; Patrick Baird and staff, Birmingham Central Library (Local Studies); Ken Kelly for the use of the colour slide on the jacket; Bill Smith for the use of his copyright photographs; Mike Vockins, Secretary of Worcestershire CCC, and his personal assistant Pauline Boyce, for all their help and advice regarding the club.

We are also grateful to: George Chesterton (former player and Committee man) of Malvern College for permission to see their collection of photographs; all the Birmingham league clubs in which Worcestershire players have on occasions played; Roly Jenkins for supplying the Afterword; Colorsport, St Peter's Street, London; Berrows Newspapers (Worcester) for the use of their copyright photographs; and Jane McNamara for her help.

Finally, we are indeed indebted to all relatives and friends of former players who have assisted with illustrations and other items of information and – last but not least – to the players themselves, without whom this book would not have been possible.

Introduction

A Brief History

That cricket is not a game 'natural' to the county of Worcester is evidenced by the fact that there is no certain reference to cricket having been played in the county before the nineteenth century, and although one or two 'Worcestershire' teams had played, somewhat unsuccessfully, in the 1830s and 1840s it is not until 1847 that incontrovertible evidence of the actual existence of a county club can be found, when it was stated to have fifty-eight members. This club merged with the Worcester City Cricket Club in 1855, but the new association failed to flourish, and despite a reorganization in 1857, by 1865 the way was cleared for the formation of a 'regularly constituted club' and in March that year the present County Cricket Club was formed and had its first meeting.

Despite aristocratic connections – Lytteltons and Coventrys abounded in the early county teams and committees – the club seemed to make little progress, and it was not until 1895, and the founding of the Minor Counties Championship that things really started moving. The county's live-wire secretary, P.H. Foley, instigated a meeting in Birmingham which led to the formation of this competition, so his county could hardly have been excluded.

The first season of the new championship emphasized that its management left much to be desired. Indeed, at the end of the season, there existed the farcical situation of Worcestershire's being awarded the title by one section of the cricket press, and Norfolk and Durham's being acclaimed joint champions elsewhere. The following three seasons left no room for doubt however; Worcestershire, the champion each time, was inarguably the strongest minor county, and it came as no surprise when in December 1898, MCC Secretary F.E. Lacey informed P.H. Foley that as from 1899 Worcestershire would be recognized as a 'first-class' county and would compete in the County Championship proper.

They certainly deserved their promotion. The Devon-born professional Ted Arnold was already an outstanding all-rounder whose success in the first-class game was to win him test honours – in spite of a suspect temperament and a liking for strong drink which probably contributed to his early decline. Batsman Fred Wheldon and the burly Dick Burrows (still playing after the Great War) were two other professionals well up to standard, while Tommy Straw was a sound wicketkeeper. The amateur element was headed by skipper Harry Foster, and in the first first-class season he received valuable batting support from two of his brothers, Wilfred and Reg. Waiting in the wings were four more Foster brothers and had they all been able to play regularly the county would have had few batting problems for the next twenty years. As it was, the service provided by the family was incalculable – not for nothing was the county christened 'Fostershire'.

Under these circumstances, the position of 12th out of fifteen in the first season was slightly disappointing. They did not have the best of luck – of five drawn matches one was ruined by rain – but Worcestershire had so much the better of three other draws that one suspects the biggest handicap was an inability to capitalize on a potentially winning position.

The county's initial Championship match – against Yorkshire – was a real 'cracker'. Inspired fast bowling by George Wilson (8–70 on his first-class debut) saw the Tykes crumble to 139 all out, and then determined batting by the two professionals Wheldon and Arnold guided the team to a lead of 72. A stubborn innings by Ted Wainwright kept Yorkshire in the game – just – but a victory target of 134 seemed a comparatively light task and Worcestershire must have scented a famous victory. Unfortunately, an inspired spell of fast bowling by a little-known professional, John Brown, from Darfield, set the home side's wickets tumbling, and they were dismissed for 122. However, this anticlimactic ending could not disguise the promise shown by the newcomers and they could reasonably have expected to finish with more than their two victories.

Unfortunately, the promise was hardly fulfilled. The seasons that followed saw the county merely holding its own, and they rarely strayed into the top half of the table, and in 1906 they subsided to 14th position out of sixteen. A mere two victories were recorded, and a glance at the averages makes the reason for their struggle obvious. The batting, with four regular players exceeding an average of 37, and Ted Arnold top of the tree at 48, was reasonable, but of the bowlers only Albert Bird averaged less than 30, with Arnold and Wilson, in particular, showing a great deterioration in form. The signs for 1907 were not good, yet the county surely exceeded its own wildest hopes, finishing equal second with Yorkshire, and including a 'double' over them among their eight victories. The batting, with eight regular players averaging more than 25, was stronger than ever, while Australian left-arm spinner John Cuffe carried all before him as he improved beyond all recognition to top the bowling.

Hopes of a continuing challenge for the top spot were soon dashed. Until the outbreak of war the county rarely strayed out of the lower echelons while the club's financial troubles, never far beneath the surface, reared up with a vengeance. In 1913 only an appeal ensured survival, and in the following year the situation was so critical that the committee put up a motion at a special general meeting that the club be wound up. Fortunately it was not carried, and during the time that the First World War occupied centre-stage the financial situation showed a big improvement.

Worcestershire did not take part in the County Championship in 1919 and so barren were the seasons which followed that it was probably questioned whether they should have returned to the fray at all. Despite the advent of a marvellous bowler in Fred Root an ever-changing side was quite unable to make any impact in the Championship, and from 1920 to 1929 they finished last on four occasions and never rose above 14th position. The nadir was reached in 1928 when their third successive season as wooden-spoonists saw them win not a single match – a desperate state of affairs which happily remains unique in the club's history.

By glancing at the averages it is not too difficult to work out reasons for the team's failure. Thirty-one players were used throughout the Championship, and on figures alone few seemed to be of the right calibre. The fact that five batsmen topped 1000 runs suggests that the batting, at least, was adequate, but only J.B. Higgins averaged 30. Fred Root achieved the 'double' but in fact had a very poor season, his batting and bowling averages being a mere 20.88 and 29.07 respectively. The second-highest wicket-taker, Victor Tarbox, averaged 39.75, which says it all. Not quite all was gloom however; 'Doc' Gibbons's first full season saw him comfortably exceed 1000 runs, while in all matches he set a new county record of 1844 runs. The manner of their making suggested a great future, but although remaining a Worcestershire stalwart until World War II he never quite regained the *élan* of his first season.

Bottom place, and no victories – the county could either go up or out, and fortunately the former was the case, though the progress made was hardly startling. In 1930 they surprisingly climbed to 10th position. They owed much to the batting of the tragic Maurice Nichol and the bowling of the veteran Fred Root and a Yorkshire-born spinner called Brook, who joined the county after making a big League reputation and took 128 wickets. Brook gave several seasons of valuable service but never reproduced his lethal first-season form, which was hardly surprising since many years later it was discovered that the singular Brook had knocked several years off his age when joining the county, and was already well into his forties!

Notwithstanding the great value of players like George Brook, it must have become obvious to the county's authorities that hopes of permanent success rested on the discovery and development of somewhat younger players. Such a policy gradually bore fruit and by the outbreak of the Second World War many such worthy and talented professionals as Reg Perks, Dick Howorth, Eddie Cooper and Peter Jackson had come to the forefront and played leading parts in the county's accession to 7th place in 1939. Also showing promise at this time was a young, local all-rounder whose enthusiasm for the game was to become even more legendary than his natural talent – Roly Jenkins.

It is arguable that no county suffered more than Worcestershire from the interruption brought by the war. A large number of their players would probably have reached their peak during the war years; certainly, in 1939 sufficient potential was manifest for hopes to be entertained of the very highest honours.

The first few seasons after the war saw the county among the leading members of the Championship competition and in 1949, the jubilee season for the club as a first-class side, they actually led the table for a while in mid-season, before fading into third place. While the batting lacked a little (only Eddie Cooper scored prolifically in a vintage season for batsmen) the attack was probably the most balanced in the country. Dick Howorth bowled as well as at any time in his career to top the averages, and Reg Perks showed pace and stamina remarkable in a 37-year-old; while Roly Jenkins showed the sort of form which established him as one of the best slow bowlers in the Championship – at a time of great spinning riches throughout the country. Jenkins' leg spinners gained him 140 championship victims and in all matches he completed the 'double'. From this distance it seems incredible that he played no tests in a series when general lack of penetration of good wickets caused a stalemate with New Zealand. In 1949 Roly took 183 first-class wickets in 1146.1 overs – a striking rate which speaks for itself.

Often in the midst of success are sown the seeds of failure, and in the 1950s saw a marked decline in the county's fortunes. The team had contained too many 'grey-beards' growing old together and replacements were difficult to find. The county searched far and wide but for the most part it was a case of quantity rather than quality, and it has to be said that some of the more notable disappointments cast doubts on the quality of both talent-spotting and coaching. Throughout the troubled 1950s, just one player stood firm: Don Kenyon held the batting together during the most difficult times, and as he gained in experience, so did the depth and breadth of his knowledge. In 1959 Peter Richardson had to be replaced as captain and Kenyon was a most popular choice as his successor – the county's first professional skipper.

Kenyon's success as leader was by no means immediate; 1959 and 1960 were both mediocre from a results point of view. But the foundations had been laid, and from 1961, when they finished in 4th place, until Kenyon's retirement in 1967, when they came 5th, Worcestershire were probably the best side in the Championship. Worcestershire were county champions twice under Kenyon, and twice runners-up. They also took to the new-fangled limited-overs cricket, reaching (but losing) two Gillette Cup finals in the same period. In fairness, the skipper had some talent to help him; Tom Graveney and Basil D'Oliveira are probably the best-known to the contemporary cricket follower. But the 'supporting cast' should not be forgotten: players such as Martin Horton, valiant all-rounder and local man, the lethal new-ball pair of Flavell and Coldwell, 'Giff' and his spinners, and Roy Booth, who proved to be a worthy inheritor of Hugo Yarnold's wicketkeeping mantle.

The county enjoyed mixed fortunes in the 1970s. The year 1971 saw them sink to 15th place in the Championship, but for the first time they won a limited-overs competition, coming top of the John Player-sponsored Sunday League, a success they did not repeat until 1987 and 1988. Useful form was showed in the other one-day competitions without anything ever being won, and as the eighties got underway it seemed a new stimulus was required. Glenn Turner could score mountains of runs; Gifford could wheel away until he became the colour of a boiled lobster; Alan Ormrod could show the cultured touch of a latter-day Tom Graveney. Yet they rarely looked like winning anything.

'Cometh the hour ...' and the man was a Lincolnshire-born graduate in Russian, Philip Neale. Neale's appointment in 1982 was not universally popular, and after an unsuccessful first two seasons which also saw the departure of Norman Gifford, among others, doubts must have been expressed in some of the darker nooks and crannies of the New Road ground. Those of little faith knew not their man; 1984 marked the beginning of a steady climb up the ladder of success and within five years Worcestershire were undisputed as the strongest county.

It would be wrong to attribute the county's success to Neale alone, though his leadership and batting have both played a big part. There has been the little matter of Graeme Hick, whose stupendous 405 not out in 1988 was perhaps the prelude to a whole orgy of records this marvellous batsman will eventually achieve. One ought not to understate the contributions of Curtis, Newport, Radford and Rhodes; all have reached England rank and could be followed by Illingworth and McEwan. Then what of Martin Weston, a marvellous 'bits and pieces' man and local to boot. Finally Botham and Dilley. Their on-field contributions have been neither as vital nor prolific as hoped, but for drumming up support and interest, and as proof of the county's ambition to get to the top of the heap, and stay there, the double signing was a master stroke.

Glossary

B	batsman
LB	leg-break bowler
LBG	leg-break and googly bowler
LFM	left-armed fast-medium bowler
LHB	left-handed batsman
LM	left-armed medium bowler
M	medium bowler
OB	off-break bowler
RAB	right-armed bowler
RAS	right-armed spin bowler
RF	right-armed fast bowler
RFM	right-armed fast-medium bowler
RHB	right-handed batsman
RM	right-armed medium-paced bowler
SB	spin bowler
SLA	left-armed slow bowler
SRA	right-armed slow bowler
U	University
W	Worcestershire
WCCC	Worcestershire County Cricket Club
WK	wicketkeeper
*	not out

Notes on statistics

Debut + year	Season of first-class debut for Worcestershire
Cap + year	Year of award of county cap
Benefit + amount + date	Season of benefit match and amount of money obtained

All details on cricket performances are for first-class matches unless otherwise stated.

Where no county is given after place of birth or death it can be taken as Worcestershire.

1

A–Z

A

ABBOTT, J.D. – B
Debut 1919 v War., Edgbaston. 3 matches for W 1919–20 (amateur).
Highest score: W 42 v War., Edgbaston 1919 (on debut).

ABELL, George Edmond Brackenbury (Sir) – RHB WK
b. Worcester, 22 June 1904; d. Marlborough, Wilts., 11 January 1989.
Educated at Marlborough & Corpus Christi College, Oxford.
 Debut 1923 v Essex, Worcester. 34 matches for W. 1923–39 (amateur).
Highest score: 131 v Som., Wells 1935.
 24 matches for Oxford U 1924–27, Blue 1924, 1926, 1927. While in
Indian Civil Service played for Europeans at Lahore (captain) 1928/29

G.E.B. Abell

J.D. Abbott

and 1929/30; played Ranji Trophy cricket for North India 1934/35 to 1941/42. Highest first-class score 210 in 225 minutes for North India v The Army, Lahore 1934/35; the first double century on Ranji Trophy debut, and the first century in the competition by a wicketkeeper or a European. Added 304 for 2nd wicket with Agha Raza, the first stand in the competition of 200 runs or more.

While in India Sir George became private secretary to Lords Wavell and Mountbatten, the last two Viceroys. On his return from India became a director of the Bank of England, and from 1964 to 1967 was First Civil Service Commissioner. J.N. Abell (Oxford U) and T.G. Abell (Free Foresters), his sons, both played first-class cricket.

ADSHEAD, Frank Hand – RHB
b. Dudley, 9 February 1894; d. Twyford Abbey, Ealing, London, 22 November 1977.

Debut 1927 v Lancs., Dudley. 2 matches for W 1927 (amateur). Highest score: W 14 v Lancs. on debut.

Played for Dudley in Birmingham League. Brother W.E. Barnie-Adshead (W).

AHL, Frank Douglas – RHB WK RAB
b. Potchefstroom, South Africa, 24 November 1907; d. Ashford Manor Golf Club, Middlesex, 3 May 1967.

Debut 1931 v New Zealanders, Worcester. 35 matches for W 1931–33 (professional). Highest score: W 43 v Surrey, Stourbridge 1932. Best bowling: W 4–44 v Yorks., Sheffield 1933.

Club cricket for Palmers Green and Birmingham League for Dudley.

F.H. Adshead

F.D. Ahl

M.L.Y. Ainsworth

J. Ainley

AINLEY, Joe – RHB WK
b. Huddersfield, Yorks. 28 October 1878; d. Sparkbrook, Birmingham, 18 November 1907.

Debut 1905 v Som., Worcester. 19 matches for W 1905–06 (professional). Highest score: W 13 v Kent, Tunbridge Wells 1905.

AINSWORTH, Michael Lionel Yeoward – RHB
b. Hooton, Ches., 13 May 1922; d. during a match at Hillingdon, London, 28 August 1978. Educated at Shrewsbury.

Debut 1948 v Kent, Dudley. 17 matches for W 1948–50 (amateur). Highest score; W 100 v War., Dudley 1948.

Played 17 first-class matches for Combined Services 1946–58, and also appeared for MCC and Free Foresters (last match 1964). Highest first-class score 137, Free Foresters v Cambridge U, Fenner's 1959. 2034 runs (24.22) and 3 centuries in first-class career.

A naval officer, reached the rank of Lt.-Commander.

ALDRIDGE, Keith John – RHB RFM
b. Evesham, W, 13 March 1935.
Debut 1956 v Sussex, Hove. 73 matches for W 1956–60 (professional; cap 1959). Highest score: 24* v Glam., Pontypridd 1960. Best bowling: 6–26 v Sussex, Hove 1958.
6 matches for Tasmania 1961/62–1963/64 while coaching; 256 wickets (23.56) in first-class career. No balled for illegal delivery twice by J.S. Buller, W v Leics., Kidderminster 1959 and again by J.F. Crapp, W v Glamorgan, Pontypridd 1960. Birmingham League cricket for Kidderminster and Walsall.
6ft 6in in height.

ALLCHURCH, Thomas – RHB OB
b. Oldswinford, nr Stourbridge, 24 April 1883; d. Halesowen 22 or 23 October 1934.
Debut 1919 v Glos., Worcester. 3 matches for W (amateur) 1919–20. Highest score: W 51 on debut 1919. Best bowling: W 5–70 v Lancs., Stourbridge 1920.
Birmingham League cricket for Stourbridge.

ALLEYNE, Hartley Leroy – RHB RFM
b. Bridgetown, Barbados, 27 February 1957. Educated at St John Baptist Secondary School, Barbados.
Debut 1980 v Glos., Worcester. 38 matches for W 1980–82. Highest score: W 72 v Lancs., Southport 1980. Best bowling: W 8–43 v Middx., Lord's 1981.

K.J. Aldridge

T. Allchurch

A.G. Archer

H.L. Alleyne

7 matches for Kent 1988–89. Played for Barbados 1978–83; Natal since 1986/87. Hat trick for W v Middx., Lord's 1981 during best bowling performance. No-balled for illegal delivery during 1982/83 season in West Indies. Birmingham League cricket for Dudley. Minor Counties Championship for Lincs. 1979; Bucks. 1984–86.

ANTON, John 'Hamish' Hugh – RHB RM
b. Kidderminster, 19 September 1926. Educated at Rugby and Caius College, Cambridge.
Debut 1950 v Som., Worcester. 4 matches for W 1950 (amateur). Highest score: W 26 on debut 1950.
10 matches Cambridge U 1949–50 (no blue). Highest first-class score: 45, Cambridge U v Sussex, Fenner's 1949. 361 first-class runs (15.69).

ARCHER, Alfred German – RHB WK
b. Richmond, Surrey, 6 December 1871; d. Seaford, Sussex, 15 July 1935. Educated at Haileybury.
Debut 1900 v Kent, Worcester. 4 matches 1900–01 (amateur). Highest score: W 12 v Leics., Leicester 1900.
Member of Lord Hawke's team to S. Africa 1898/99 – made first-class debut v S. Africa, Cape Town in April 1899 in match subsequently regarded as a 'test match'. Scored 7 and 24* in his only 'test'. Toured as a Shropshire amateur. Best first-class score 43, PF Warner's XI v Philadelphians 1903, his final first-class match. 231 runs (11.00) and 12 dismissals in 12 first-class matches.

ARGENT, E. – RHB OB
b. 6 February 1902.

Debut 23 May 1928 v Middlesex, Worcester. 2 matches for W 1928 (professional). Highest score: W 19 v Essex, Leyton.

ARNOLD, Edward George – RHB RFM

b. Exmouth, Devon, 7 November 1876; d. Worcester, 25 October 1942.

Debut 1899 v Yorks., Worcester. 301 matches for W 1899–1913 (professional); benefit 1912. Highest score: W 215 v Oxford U, Oxford 1910. Best bowling: W 9–64 v Oxford U, Oxford 1905. 1000 runs W (7) – 1767 (50.48) 1906 best. 100 wickets W (2) – 124 (17.33) 1903 best. 1000 runs/100 wickets 'double' for W 1903 – 1040 runs (31.51); 124 wkts (17.33). 'Doubles' in all first-class matches 1902, 1903, 1904, 1905. Bowled unchanged with J.A. Cuffe throughout match – v Yorks., Bradford 1907; Arnold 7–66, Cuffe 13–76. 'Match double' v War.,

E.G. Arnold

J.R. Ashman

Edgbaston 1909 (200* 10 wkts for 114). Added 393 for 5th wicket, W v War., Edgbaston 1909, with W.B. Burns. Remains best 5th wicket stand in all first-class cricket in England.

10 test matches for England, 1903/04 to 1907. 160 runs (13.33); 31 wkts (25.41). 8 ct. First-class career record 15853 runs (29.91); 187 ct. 1069 wickets (23.16). Played for Devon before joining W. Birmingham League Cricket for Stourbridge.

ASHMAN, John Robert – LHB SLA

b. Rotherham, Yorks., 20 May 1926.

Debut 1953 v Australians, Worcester. 33 matches for W 1953–54 (professional). Highest score: W 24 v Derbys., Derby 1953. Best bowling: W 7–111 v Oxford U, Oxford 1954.

1 match for Yorks., 1951.

Clubs included Bowling Old Lane (Bradford League, Sheffield). Brother Allan Ashman soccer for Carlisle United and soccer manager, Carlisle United and West Bromwich Albion.

ASHTON, Gilbert – RHB SLA

b. Bromley, Kent, 29 September 1896. d. Abberley, W, 6 February 1981. Educated at Winchester and Trinity College, Cambridge.

Debut 1922 v Notts., Worcester. 27 matches for W 1922–36 (amateur). Highest score: W 125 v Northants, Worcester 1922. On W committee and President 1967–69.

Played Cambridge U 1919–21; Blue each year, captain 1921. Rarely bowled, but took 3–49, Cambridge v Royal Navy, Fenner's 1919. 2329 runs (24.01) in first-class career. Birmingham League cricket for Kidderminster.

Brothers were Sir Hubert Ashton (Cambridge and Essex), C.T. Ashton (Cambridge and Essex), P. Ashton (Essex). G. Ashton won soccer Blue at Cambridge. Won Military Cross in World War I, and lost a thumb. For many years headmaster of Abberley Hall Prep. School.

AUSTIN, Harry – LHB SLA

b. Moseley, Birmingham, 17 April 1892; d. Canterbury, Kent, 28 August 1968. Educated at Tindall Street School.

Debut 1928 v Yorks., Hull. 2 matches for W 1928. (professional). Highest score: W 9 v Som., Taunton 1928. Best bowling: 1–41 same match.

4 matches for War. 1919. Professional for Kidderminster (Birmingham League). Later coach and groundsman.

G. Ashton

H. Austin

BACHE, Harold Godfrey – LHB SLA

b. Churchill, W 20 August 1889; d. in action, Comines Canal Bank, Ypres, Belgium, 15 February 1916. Educated at King Edward VI Grammar School, Birmingham and Caius College, Cambridge.

Debut 1907 v Surrey, Worcester, while still at school. 17 matches for W 1907–10 (amateur). Highest score: W 36 v Middx., Lord's 1909. Rarely bowled, but took 2–4 in innings v Middx., Worcester 1910.

Played Cambridge U 1909–10, without winning blue. 270 first-class runs (9.00); 3 wkts for 39 runs. Birmingham League cricket for West Bromwich Dartmouth.

Soccer – centre forward for West Bromwich Albion; 7 amateur caps for England 1910–13. Cambridge Blue for soccer, also played lawn tennis for Cambridge.

E.S. Baker

H.F. Baker

E.W. Bale

D.A. Banks

BAKER, Edward Stanley – RHB WK
b. Moseley, Birmingham, 9 November 1910. Educated at King Edward's School, Birmingham.
    Debut 1933 v Glos., Cheltenham. 32 matches for W 1933–34 (amateur). Highest score: W 21* v Sussex, Worcester 1934.

BAKER, Harold Frank – RHB SLA
b. Walsall, Staffs., 4 May 1884; d. Hagley, W, 4 May 1954.
    Debut 1911 v Essex, Stourbridge. 2 matches for W 1911 (amateur). Highest score: W 8* v Glos., Dudley 1911.
    Birmingham League cricket for Dudley.

BAKER, W.
Debut 1920 v Essex, Leyton. 2 matches for W 1920 (amateur). Highest score: W 7 on debut. Best bowling: W 1–38 on debut.

BALE, Ernest William – RHB WK
b. Mitcham, Surrey, 18 September 1876; d. Carshalton, Surrey, 6 July 1952.
    Debut 1908 v MCC, Lord's. 138 matches for W 1908–20 (professional). Highest score: W 43 v S. Africa, Worcester 1912. 6 dismissals in an innings (2 ct 4 st) v Australia, Worcester 1909. W record until beaten by H. Yarnold in 1951.
    1 match for Surrey 1904, 6 matches for London County 1904.

BANKS, David Andrew – RHB RM
b. Pensnett, Staffs., 11 January 1961. Educated at Pensnett Secondary

School; Dudley Technical College.

Debut 1983 v Oxford U, Oxford. 19 matches for W 1983–85. Highest score W 100 v Oxford U, Oxford 1983 on debut (only second batsman to score century for W on first-class debut).

11 matches for War. 1988–89. Played Staffs. in Minor Counties Championship 1986–88. Birmingham League cricket for Stourbridge, Old Hill and West Bromwich Dartmouth.

BANNISTER, Arthur Frederick – B SB

b. Somers Town, London, 15 June 1875; d. Islington, London, 17 November 1958.

Debut 1900 v Yorks., Bradford. 38 matches for W 1900–02 (professional). Highest score: W 44 v S. Africa, Worcester 1901. Best bowling: W 7–29 v Hampshire, Worcester 1900.

Played Birmingham League cricket for Kidderminster.

(NB Other sources differ with regard to personal details; the above is correct.)

BARKER, Anthony 'Royston' Paul – RHB OB

b. Maybank, Newcastle-under-Lyme, Staffs., 30 May 1947.

Debut 1967 v Kent, Tunbridge Wells. 27 matches for W 1967–69. Highest score: W 67 v Lancs., Southport 1969.

Played Birmingham League cricket for Dudley, Walsall, Kidderminster, Duport. Also professional for Burslem. Played Staffs. in Minor Counties 1970.

A.R.P. Barker

W.E. Barnie-Adshead

B.J. Barrett

BARLEY, Jack Charles – RHB WK
b. Eton, Bucks., 4 December 1887; d. Surfers' Paradise, Queensland, Australia about 1960. Educated at Tonbridge and Oxford.
   Debut 1909 v Oxford U, Oxford. 1 match for W 1909 (amateur). Highest score: 1* above.
   1 match Sussex 1908, 1 match Oxford U 1909, 1 match Leveson Gower's XI 1909.

BARNIE-ADSHEAD, William Ewart – RHB
b. Dudley, 10 April 1901; d. Edgbaston, Birmingham, 26 January 1951.
   Debut 1922 v Sussex, Worcester. 12 matches for W 1922–28 (amateur). Highest score: 51 v War., Edgbaston 1925.
   Played for Dudley in Birmingham League.
   Played soccer for Aston Villa. A medical practitioner. Brother F.H. Adshead (W).

BARRETT, Brian Joseph – RHB RFM
b. Auckland, New Zealand, 16 November 1966. Educated at Edgewater College, Auckland.
   Debut 1985 v Cambridge U, Cambridge. 1 match for W 1985 – did not bat; 1 wicket.
   Played for Auckland (New Zealand) 1985/86; Northern Districts since 1986/87. Best first-class bowling: 4–41 Northern Districts v Central Districts, Te Awamutu, 1987/88. Highest first-class score: 25* v Auckland, Auckland 1987/88. Birmingham League cricket for Dudley.

E.H. Bennett

E.G. Bayliss

BAYLIS, Keith Rodney – RHB LB
b. Redditch, 5 November 1947. Educated at Ellesmere College.
   Debut 1966 v Cambridge U, Cambridge 1966. 6 matches for W 1966–67. Highest score: W 26 on debut 1966. Best bowling: W 4–112 v Essex, Worcester 1967.
   Birmingham League cricket for Mitchells & Butlers.

BAYLISS, Edward George – RHB
b. Worcester, 5 January 1918.
   Debut 1939 v Leics., Leicester. 1 match W 1939 (amateur). 0 runs in either innings.
   Birmingham League cricket for Old Hill.

BENNETT, Enoch Harvey – RHB
b. Dudley, 21 December 1894.
   Debut 1925 v War., Edgbaston. 3 matches W 1925 (amateur). Highest score: W 10 v Yorks., Worcester 1925.
   First-class match for Civil Service v New Zealand at Chiswick 1927, scoring 73 and 60 (top score in each innings).
Played Staffs. (Minor Counties) 1921–22.

BENNETT, Hugh Frederic
b. Pershore, W, 10 November 1862; d. Malvern, 26 July 1943. Educated at Bradfield.
   Debut 1901 v Glos., Bristol. 2 matches W 1901 (amateur). Highest

score: W 31 on debut.
  Church of England vicar.

BENNETT, M.
Debut 1946 v Combined Services, Worcester. 1 match W 1946. Highest
score: W 8 in only match.

BENT, Paul – RHB OB
b. Worcester, 1 May 1965. Educated at Worcester Royal Grammar
School.
  Debut 1985 v Cambridge U, Cambridge. 17 matches for W 1985–date.
Highest score: W 144 v Kent, Worcester 1989.
  Birmingham League cricket for Worcester City.

BERKELEY, Robert George Wilmot – RHB
b. Romford, Essex, 23 April 1898; d. Bristol, 28 August 1969. Educated
at Downside and Magdalen College, Oxford.
  Debut 1919 v H.K. Foster's XI, Hereford. 4 matches for W 1919–22.
Highest score: 16 v H.K. Foster's XI, Worcester 1919.

BERRY, Robert – LHB SLA
b. Manchester, 29 January 1926.
  Debut 1955 v S. Africa, Worcester. 94 matches for W 1955–58

P. Bent

R. Berry

(professional). Cap 1957. Highest score: W 32 v Som., Worcester 1957. Best bowling: W 6–37 v Glos., Bristol 1956 (took 11–101 in match).

Played 93 matches Lancs. 1948–54 (Cap 1950) and 54 matches Derby. 1959–62 (Cap 1961). First player to be capped by three counties. Best bowling in innings in first-class cricket: 10–102 (14–125 match), Lancs v W, Blackpool 1953. Also took 14–125 match, Lancs. v Somerset, Old Trafford 1953. Two test matches, England v W. Indies 1950. Test record: 6 runs (3.00); 9 wickets for 228 runs (25.33). Best test bowling 5–63 on debut, Old Trafford 1950. Toured Australia with MCC 1950/51; Commonwealth team to India 1953/54. 703 wickets (24.73) in first-class career.

A well-known breeder and racer of pigeons.

BEVINS, Stuart Roy – RHB WK
b. Solihull, West Midlands, 8 March 1967. Educated at Solihull.

Debut 1989 v Notts., Worcester. 2 matches for W 1989. Highest score: W 6* v Notts., Worcester on debut.

Birmingham League cricket for Walsall.

BIRD, Albert – RHB OB
b. Moseley, Birmingham, 17 August 1867; d. Worcester, 17 June 1927.

Debut 1899 v Yorks., Worcester. 143 matches W 1899–1909

S.R. Bevins

A. Bird

R.E. Bird

J. Birkenshaw

(professional). Highest score: W 64* v Lancs., Worcester 1902. Best bowling: W 7–41 v Oxford U, Oxford 1903. Match figures of 14–109 (7–53, 7–56) v Hants, Southampton 1901.

Played Warwickshire (pre-first-class) 1887–90; W (pre-first-class) from 1892. Birmingham League cricket for Walsall. An accomplished amateur musician.

Brother William Bird played War. and W in pre-first-class matches; Cousins – Jimmy Windridge (War. CCC, Chelsea, Middlesbrough, Birmingham soccer clubs), Jack Leake (War. pre-first-class), Albert Leake (Aston Villa and England soccer player).

BIRD, Ronald Ernest – RHB RMF

b. Quarry Bank, Staffs., 4 April 1915; d. Feckenham, W, 20 February 1985.

Debut 1946 v India, Worcester. 190 matches W 1946–54; Cap 1946; Captain 1952–54 (amateur). Highest score: W 158* v Som., Taunton 1952. Best bowling: W 3–39 v Cambridge U, Worcester 1949. 1000 runs (3) 1591 (37.00) 1952 best.

Played for Moseley, Stourbridge, Old Hill in Birmingham League.

BIRKENSHAW, Jack – LHB ROB

b. Rothwell, Leeds, 13 November 1940. Educated at Rothwell Grammar School.

Debut 1981 v Sussex, Worcester. 10 matches W 1981. Highest score: W 54 v Australia, Worcester 1981. Best bowling: W 3–131 v Derby., Chesterfield 1981.

30 matches for Yorks. 1958–60 (professional); 420 matches Leics. 1961–80 (originally professional); Cap 1965, Benefit (£13,100) 1974. 5 test matches for England 1972/73–1973/74. 146 runs (21.14); highest score: 64 v India, Kanpur 1972/73; 13 wickets (36.07); best bowling: 5–57 v Pakistan, Karachi 1972/73 in test cricket. 100 wickets in a season (2) – 111 (21.41) in 1967 best. 2 first-class 'hat tricks' – for Leics., v W, Worcester 1967, and v Cambridge U, Fenner's 1968. Full first-class career record: 12780 runs (23.57); 1073 wickets (27.28); 318 catches. Highest first-class score: 131, Leics. v Surrey, Guildford 1969; Best first-class bowling: 8–94 Leics. v Som., Taunton 1972.

First-class umpire 1982–88. Umpired two test matches 1986, 1988. Joined Somerset coaching staff 1989.

BLAKEY, George Matthew – RHB RAB
b. St Anne's on Sea, Lancs., 20 January 1907; d. Meir, Stoke-on-Trent, 12 January 1968.

Debut 1939 v Surrey, Worcester. 3 matches W 1939 (professional). Highest score: W 42 v Surrey, Worcester, on debut.

Birmingham League cricket for Dudley and Kidderminster. County cricket for Salop.

BLEWITT, Charles Percy – RHB
b. Kates Hill, Dudley, 15 October 1877; d. Danesford, Salop., 15 December 1937.

Debut 1912 v Kent, Dudley. 1 match W (amateur) 1912. Highest score: W 4 on debut.

G.M. Blakey

C.P. Blewitt

R. Booth

L. Blunt

BLUNT, Leonard – RHB RFM

b. Worcester, 29 March 1921. Educated at St John's School, Worcester.

Debut 1946 v Hants, Southampton. 14 matches for W 1946–48 (professional). Highest score: W 18 v Combined Services, Worcester 1946. Best bowling: W 5–60 v Hants, Southampton 1946.

Made first-class debut for Europeans v India, Madras Presidency 1942/43. Played for Ches. (Minor Counties) 1950–53 while professional for Nantwich.

BOOTH, Roy – RHB WK

b. Marsden, Yorks., 1 October 1926.

Debut 1956 v Australia, Worcester. 402 matches W 1956–70 (professional). Cap 1956; Benefit (£6,240) 1966. Highest score: W 113* v Sussex, Hove 1959. 101 dismissals (85 ct 16 st) in 1960, 100 dismissals (90 ct 10 st) in 1964. 8 catches in match, v Essex, Romford 1962 – W record until 1988. 1015 dismissals (868 ct 147 st) for W – county record. On W CCC committee.

Played 65 matches for Yorks. 1951–55. 10138 first-class runs (18.87); 1126 dismissals (949 ct, 177 st).

BOTHAM, Ian Terence – RHB RFM/RM
b. Heswall, Ches., 24 November 1955. Educated at Buckler's Mead Secondary School, Yeovil.

Debut 1987 v Kent, Worcester. 29 matches for W 1987–date (cap 1987). Highest score: W 126* v Som., Taunton 1987. Best bowling: W 7–85 v Sussex, Hove 1989.

172 matches for Som. 1974–86 (cap 1976); captain 1984–85; benefit 1984. Played for Queensland 1987/88: dismissed after one season. 97 tests for England, 1977–89; captain 12 times. Highest test score: 208 v India, The Oval 1982. Best test bowling: 8–34 v Pakistan, Lord's 1978. test career record: 5119 runs (34.35); 14 centuries, 112 catches; 376 wickets (28.27).

Highest first-class score 228, Som. v Glos., Taunton 1980. Best first-class bowling – as in tests. First-class career figures: 16841 runs (34.02); 1061 wickets (26.76). Achieved 100 Test wickets in 2 years, 9 days, and 200 test wickets in 4 years, 34 days – both records. Test 'double' and 2000 run/200 wicket 'double' in 21 and 42 tests respectively – both records. First to complete 3000/300 test 'double'. First test player to

I.T. Botham

J.J. Bowles

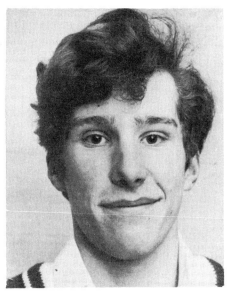

F.L. Bowley

C.N. Boyns

score century and take 8 wickets in innings in a match – v Pakistan, Lord's 1978. In 1979/80, at Bombay v India, became first test player to score a century and take 10 wickets in a match. Scored 122 in 58 minutes from 55 balls, England XI v Central Zone, Indore 1981/82, reaching century in 50 minutes. During 131*, Somerset v War., Taunton 1982, reached century in 52 minutes from 56 balls. Scored 32 runs from one over bowled by I.R. Snook. England XI v Central Districts, Palmerston North 1983/84, and 30 from 1 over bowled by Paul Smith, Som. v War., Taunton 1982. Holds the Som. records for 4th wicket – 310 with P. Denning 1980 – and 8th wicket – 172 with I.V.A. Richards 1983. Hit 80 first-class sixes in 1985 – a record for a season.

Back operation in 1988 has hindered his subsequent cricketing activities.

BOWLES, John Jesse – RHB SLA
b. Lower Slaughter, Glos., 3 April 1890; d. Salisbury, 27 November 1971.

Debut 1926 v Lancs., Old Trafford. 62 matches for W 1926–28 (professional). Highest score: W 73 v Glos., Cheltenham 1926. Best bowling: W 5–56 v Sussex, Hove 1926.

18 matches for Glos. 1911–20. 1392 first-class runs (11.50); 83 wickets (41.65). Played as club professional for Enfield (C Lancs. League). Birmingham League cricket for Kidderminster and Old Hill.

BOWLEY, Frederick Lloyd – RHB
b. Brecon, Wales, 9 November 1873; d. Worcester, 31 May 1943.

Debut 1899 v Sussex, Hove 1899. 396 matches for W 1899–1923 (professional). Highest score: W 276 v Hants, Dudley 1914 (county record until beaten by Glenn Turner in 1982). 1000 runs in season (14) – 1628 (41.74) 1906 best. Holds W record 1st wicket partnership record with H.K. Foster – 309 v Derbys., Derby 1901. Also added 306 for 1st wicket with F.A. Pearson, v Glos., Worcester 1913. Carried bat through innings – 104*/267 v Middx, Lord's 1911. 100 before lunch on first morning of match on six occasions – W record. Scored 21122 first-class runs (29.62) and scored 38 centuries.

Played Heanor CC and Derbys Colts aged 14. Coached at Repton, Haileybury and St Paul's Schools.

BOYNS, Cedric Nigel – RHB RM

b. Harrogate, Yorks. 14 August 1954. Educated at Adams Grammar School, Newport, Salop., London U and Hughes Hall, Cambridge U.

Debut 1976 v Lancs., Worcester. 33 matches W 1976–79. Highest score: W 95 v Yorks., Scarborough 1976. Best bowling: W 3–24 v Oxford U, Oxford 1977.

Played 4 matches Cambridge U 1976. Played Birmingham League cricket for Old Hill. Minor Counties cricket for Salop., 1973–85.

BRADLEY, Michael Ewart – RHB SLA

b. Stourbridge, 29 March 1934. Educated at Halesowen Technical College.

Debut 1951 v Combined Services, Worcester. 9 matches for W (professional) 1951–52. Highest score: W 6* v Scotland, Dundee 1951. Best bowling: W 6–162 v Notts., Dudley 1952.

Played Old Hill in Birmingham League, and for Halesowen in Midlands Club Cricket Conference.

BRAIN, Brian Maurice – RHB RFM

b. Worcester, 13 September 1940. Educated at King's School, Worcester.

Debut 1959 v Oxford U, Worcester. 149 matches for W (initially as professional) 1959–75. Cap 1966. Highest score: W 38 v Glos., Cheltenham 1964. Best bowling: W 8–55 v Essex, Worcester 1975. Toured Rhodesia in 1964/65 and Jamaica 1965/66, each time with W.

110 first-class matches for Glos. 1976–81 (cap 1977). Highest first-class score: 57 for Glos. v Essex, Cheltenham 1976. Birmingham League cricket for Stourbridge, West Bromwich Dartmouth and Old Hill.

Author, *Another Day. Another Match* (1981).

BRINTON, Percival Robert – RHB

b. Kidderminster, 5 February 1873; d. Oxford, 14 May 1958. Educated at Winchester.

B.M. Brain   *R.G. Broadbent*

Debut 1904 v Oxford U, Oxford. 1 match for W (amateur) 1904. Scored 1 run, only innings.

BRINTON, Ronald Lewis – RHB
b. Kidderminster, 26 February 1903; d. Malvern, 19 April 1980. Educated at Shrewsbury.
    Debut 1924 v War., Kidderminster. 2 matches for W (amateur) 1924. Highest score W 10 v Notts., Trent Bridge 1924.
    Birmingham League cricket for Kidderminster.

BRINTON, Reginald Seymour – RHB RFM
b. Lower Mitton, W, 15 December 1869; d. Kidderminster, 23 February 1942. Educated at Winchester and Oxford U.
    Debut 1903 v Yorks, Worcester. 13 matches for W 1903–09 (amateur). Highest score: W 72* v Oxford U, Worcester 1904.
    Birmingham League cricket for Kidderminster.
    Brother P.R. Brinton (W).

BROADBENT, Robert Gillespie – RHB RMF
b. Beckenham, Kent, 21 June 1924. Educated at Caterham School.
    Debut 1950 v Leics., Leicester, scoring 77 and 29*. 307 matches for W 1950–63 (professional). Cap 1951; benefit (£5,402) 1961. Highest score W 155 v Middx., Worcester 1951. 1000 runs (7); 1556 (33.10) 1952 best.
    Played Minor Counties for Hertfordshire 1964. Birmingham League cricket for West Bromwich Dartmouth.

BROMLEY-MARTIN, Eliot George – RHB RAS
b. Worcester, 8 October 1866; d. Walton, Radnorshire, 23 January 1946.
Educated at Eton and New College, Oxford U.

Debut 1899 v Yorks., Worcester (after previous appearances in non-first-class matches). 10 matches for W (amateur) 1899–1900. Highest score: W 39 v Leics., Leicester 1899. Best bowling: W 4–33 v Yorks., Worcester 1899. Hon. Sec. W 1886–88.

Brother G.E. Bromley-Martin (W).

BROMLEY-MARTIN, Granville Edward – RHB RAS
b. Callow End, W, 18 October 1875; d. Hassocks, Sussex, 31 May 1941.
Educated at Eton (Captain 1893, 1894) and New College, Oxford U.

Debut 1899 v Yorks, Worcester. 32 matches for W 1899–1904 (amateur). Highest score: W 129 v Derbys., Worcester 1899.

Played Oxford U 1897–98; Blue each season. Highest first-class score 137, Oxford U v Sussex, Hove 1897. First-class career record – 1779 runs (21.69).

Brother E.G. Bromley-Martin (W).

G.E. Bromley-Martin

E.G. Bromley-Martin

A. Brown

BROOK, George Wilfred – RHB SLA
b. Mirfield, Yorks., 30 August 1888; d. Bournemouth, Hants, 24 July 1966.

Debut 1930 v Australia, Worcester. 150 matches for W 1930–35 (professional). Cap 1930. Highest score: W 56 v Glos., Worcester 1933. Best bowling: W 7–50 (12–90 match) v Leics., Leicester 1930. 132 wickets (21.88) 1930.

Birmingham League cricket for Kidderminster (professional). Professional for Keighley before and after first-class career, later Bowling Old Lane in Bradford League.

Knocked 7 years off age when making debut for W; correct age was 41.

BROWN, Alan – RHB WK
b. Darwen, Lancs., 23 December 1957. Educated at Darwen Grammar School, St John's College, York U.

Debut 1979 v Oxford U, Oxford. 1 match 1979 – did not bat.

BROWNELL, Eric Lindsay Douglas – RHB

b. Hobart, Tasmania, 7 November 1876; d. Windsor, New South Wales, 22 October 1945.

Debut 1908 v Oxford U, Oxford. 1 match for W 1980 (amateur). Scored 21 and 7.

BRYANT, Edwin Harvey – B

b. Bromsgrove, 12 September 1886; d. Barnt Green, 24 October 1948.

Debut 1923 v Yorks., Worcester. 16 matches W 1923–25 (amateur). Highest score: 63 v Essex, Leyton 1924.

Birmingham League cricket for Stourbridge.

BULL, Charles Harry – RHB

b. Lewisham, Kent, 29 March 1909; d. in traffic accident at Margaretting, Chelmsford, Essex, 28 May 1939.

Debut 1931 v New Zealand, Worcester. 171 matches for W 1931–39 (professional); capped. Highest score: W 161 v Glam., Cardiff. 1000 runs (4), 1619 (28.40), 1937 best.

4 first-class matches for Kent 1929–30. Birmingham League professional for Dudley.

Was top-class table-tennis player.

E.H. Bryant

C.H. Bull

E.L. Bunting

J.S. Buller

BULLER, John Sydney – RHB WK
b. Wortley, Bramley, Yorks, 23 August 1909; d. Edgbaston, Birmingham while umpiring first-class match, 7 August 1970.
   Debut 1935 v S Africa, Worcester 1935. 110 matches for W (professional) 1935–46. Highest score: W 64 v Northants, Kettering 1938. 247 dismissals (176 ct 71 st) for W.
   1 match for Yorks. 1930.
   First-class umpire 1951–70; (33 tests 1956–69). Awarded MBE 1965 for Services to Umpiring.

BULLOCK, Mark – B
b. Dudley, 1872; d. Leicester, 22 April 1925.
   Debut 1900 v Leics., Worcester. 4 matches for W (professional) 1900. Highest score: W 27 on debut.
   Birmingham League for Dudley.

BULLOCK, Percy George – RHB SLA
b. Birmingham, 28 August 1893; d. Wythall, 1 December 1986.
   Debut v Essex, Leyton 1921. 3 matches for W (professional) 1921. Highest score: W 9 v Derby., Worcester 1921.

BUNTING, Edward Lancelot – RHB RM
b. Tillington, Staffs., 10 December 1883; d. Barnwood, Glos., 26 February 1962. Educated at Blundell's School.
   Debut 1922 v Yorks., Dudley. 1 match for W 1922 (amateur). Highest score: W 1 v Yorks., Dudley 1922.
   A medical practitioner.

BURLTON, Arthur Temple ('Bobbie') – RHB OB
b. Coimbatore, India, 10 March 1900; d. Ballochneck, Thornhill, Stirling, Scotland, 10 February 1980. Educated at Repton.

Debut 1922 v Sussex, Hove. 5 matches for W (amateur) 1922. Highest score: W 35* v Glam., Cardiff 1922.

Author *Cricketing Courtesy* (Bromsgrove Messenger, 1954).

BURNS, William Beaumont – RHB RF
b. Rugeley, Staffs., 29 August 1883; d. Contalmaison, France, in action, 7 July 1916. Educated at King's School, Ely.

Debut 1903 v Oxford U, Oxford. 196 matches for W 1903–13 '(amateur). Highest score: W 196 v War., Edgbaston 1909. Best bowling: W 6–41 v Som., Taunton 1913 (last first-class match). 1000 runs (3) 1364 (31.10) 1911 best. Hat-trick, W v Glos., Worcester 1913.

Toured New Zealand with MCC party, 1906/07. Innings analysis of 7-58, Gentlemen v Players, The Oval 1910, best first-class figures. First-class career record: 9479 runs (27.00); 214 wickets (29.59). Played Staffs. 1901–02.

Bowler of considerable pace, but action sometimes considered dubious.

W.B. Burns

R.D. Burrows

BURR, Frederick Bonham – RHB

b. Hastings, Sussex, 2 August 1887; d. in action, Kemmel, Belgium, 12 March 1915. Educated at Denstone and Keble College, Oxford U.

Debut 1911 v Oxford U, Oxford. Scored 39 and 7* in only first-class match.

BURROWS, Robert Dixon – RHB RF

b. Eastwood, Notts., 6 June 1871; d. Hill Top, Eastwood, Notts, 12 February 1943.

Debut 1899 v Yorks., Worcester. 277 matches for W (professional) 1899–1919. Highest score: W 112 v Glos., Worcester 1907. Best bowling: W 8–48 v Som., Taunton 1908. 100 (2); 100 (23.46) 1910; 100 (21.41) 1913.

Birmingham League cricket for Stourbridge. Sent bail 67 yards, 6 inches when bowling W. Huddleston, Lancs., Old Trafford 1911.

First-class umpire 1923–31.

BUSHER, Sydney Edmund – RHB RFM

b. Solihull, War. 19 December 1882; d. Turramurra, New South Wales, Australia, May 1953.

Debut 1908 v Glos., Bristol. 4 matches for W 1908–10 (amateur). Highest score: W 18* v Som, Taunton 1910. Best bowling: W 6–63 v Glos., Bristol 1908.

Played 1 match, Surrey v Gentleman, The Oval 1908.

Brother H.A. Busher played War.

BYRNE, George Robert – RHB RM

b. Northfield, Birmingham, 28 May 1892; d. Torteval, Guernsey, 23 June 1973. Educated at Downside.

Debut 1914 v Leics., Coalville. 4 matches for W (amateur) 1914-21. Highest score: W 18 v Leics., Coalville 1914. Best bowling: W 1–86 same match.

Played 8 matches for War. 1912. Best first-class analysis 3–9 (including 3 wickets in 4 balls), War. v Middx., Edgbaston 1912. Played for Moseley in Birmingham League.

Uncle J.F. Byrne (War.).

CALDWELL, William Somerville – RHB
b. Altrincham, Ches., 26 February 1878; d. Littlemore, Oxon., 14 January 1964.

Debut 1901 v Kent, Worcester. 20 matches for W 1901–04 (amateur). Highest score: W 133 v Sussex, Worcester 1903. Best bowling: 2–23 v War., Edgbaston 1904.

Was a Church of England priest.

CARMICHAEL, Evelyn George Massey (Carmichael of Carmichael) – RHB RM
b. Worcester, 3 April 1871; d. Berrington, Shrewsbury, 14 July 1959. Educated at Harrow and Oxford U.

Debut v Oxford U, Oxford 1903.

6 runs in only 2 first-class innings.

A.M. Carr   *R.G.M. Carter*

G.R. Cass

CARR, Austin Michael – RHB
b. Chester, 29 September 1898; d. Great Witley, W, 20 December 1946.
Educated at Eton.
    Debut 1921 v Essex, Worcester. 6 matches for W 1921–25 (amateur).
Highest score: W 82 v Essex, Worcester 1922 (debut).
    Headmaster of Abberley Hall School, Abberley.

CARTER, Robert George Mallaby – LHB RFM
b. Horden, Co. Durham, 11 July 1937. Educated at Nunthorpe Grammar
School, York.
    Debut 1961 v Oxford U, Worcester. 177 for matches W, 1961–72; Cap
1965. Originally a professional. Highest score: W 23 v Leics., Leicester
1967. Best bowling: W 7–61 v Yorks., Dudley 1971.
    Birmingham League cricket for Dudley and Stourbridge.
    A leading national cricket coach.

CASS, George Rodney – LHB WK
b. Overton, Yorks., 23 April 1940. Educated at Dewsbury Technical
College.
    Debut 1969 v W. Indies, Worcester. 104 matches for W, 1969–75
(professional); Cap 1970. Highest score: W 172* v Leics., Leicester 1975.
6 catches in innings v Essex, 1973, equalling W county championship
record.
    45 matches for Essex, 1964–67. 6 matches for Tasmania, 1970/71–1971/

72. Played Shrops. 1976–81. First-class career record; 4304 runs (21.84). Birmingham League cricket for Worcester City.

CAVE-ROGERS, Rupert Ashby – RHB
b. Cannock, Staffs., 27 May 1902; d. Eastbourne, Sussex, 2 May 1976. Educated at Malvern.
Debut v War., Edgbaston 1919 (amateur). Scored 3, only innings of only match.

CHADD, John Etheridge – RHB OB
b. Whitestone, Hereford, 27 October 1933. Educated at Hereford Cathedral School.
Debut 1955 v Scotland, Glasgow. 2 matches for W 1955–56 (professional). Highest score: W 4 v Oxford U, Worcester 1956. Best bowling: W 2–84 same match. Became Worcs committee member after playing days.
Club cricket for Hereford City CC.

R.A. Cave-Rogers

J.E. Chadd

G.H. Chesterton

F. Chester

CHATHAM, Charles Henry – RHB RM
b. Tewkesbury, Glos., 18 June 1910. Educated at Wycliffe.

Debut 1934 v Oxford U, Oxford. 1 match for W 1934 (amateur). Scored 8 and 4 in only match.

CHESTER, Frank – LHB SLA
b. Bushey, Herts., 20 January 1895; d. Bushey, 8 April 1957.

Debut 1912 v S. Africa, Worcester. 54 matches for W 1912–14 (professional). Highest score: W 178* v Essex, Worcester. Best bowling: W 6–43 v Hants, Southampton 1913. First century 115 v Som., Worcester 1913 aged 18½; youngest W century-maker until D.N. Patel.

Lost an arm in World War I; became first-class umpire 1921–55. Umpired 48 test matches, 1924–55.

CHESTERTON, George Herbert – RHB RM
b. Chirbury, Shrops., 15 July 1922. Educated at Malvern and Brasenose College, Oxford U.

Debut 1950 v Essex, Worcester 1950. 47 matches for W (amateur) 1950–57; cap 1950. Highest score: W 23 v Lancs., Old Trafford 1950. Best bowling: W 6–59 v Som., Worcester 1950.

Played 12 matches for Oxford U 1949 and won Blue. Highest first-class score 43, Oxford U v Free Foresters, Oxford 1949. Best first-class bowling 7–14, MCC v Ireland, Dublin 1956. Toured Canada with MCC 1951. First-class record; 598 runs (8.79); 263 wickets (22.78). Played Corn. 1948–49.

CLARE, Thomas – RHB
b. Brierley Hill, Staffs., 20 August 1883; d. Hagley, 6 May 1940.
Debut 1920 v Lancs., Stourbridge. 2 matches W 1920–25 (amateur).
Highest score: W 34 on debut.
Birmingham League cricket for Stourbridge.

CLIFF, Alfred Talbot – RHB SLA
b. Glanford Brigg, Lincs., 27 October 1878; d. Oxford, 25 January 1966.
Debut 1912 v Kent, Dudley. 39 matches for W 1912–20 (amateur).
Highest score: W 81* v War., Edgbaston 1919. Best bowling: W 1–4 v
Derby., Derby 1914.

COBHAM, 9th Viscount (John Cavendish Lyttelton) – RHB
b. Hagley Hall, 23 October 1881; d. Bromsgrove, 31 July 1949. Educated
at Eton.
Debut 1924 v Notts., Worcester. 3 matches for W 1924–25 (amateur).
Highest score: W 30 v War., Worcester 1925. W President at time of
death.
Father C.G. Lyttelton (Cambridge U); son C.J. Lyttelton (Cambridge
U, Worcs). MP (Droitwich) 1910–16. Secretary of State for War
1939–40. MCC Treasurer.

T. Clare

A.T. Cliff

L.J. Coldwell

COLDWELL, Leonard John – RHB RFM
b. Newton Abbot, Devon; 10 January 1933.
   Debut 1955 v Oxford U, Oxford 1955. 296 matches for W (professional) 1955–69; cap 1959; benefit (£7,502) 1968. Highest score: W 37 v Notts., Worcester 1962. Best bowling: W 8–38, v Surrey, Worcester 1962. Hat trick, W v Leics., Stourbridge 1957, and W v Essex, Brentwood 1965. 100 wickets (2) – 140 (19.25) 1961 best.
   Tours: W to Rhodesia 1964/65, Jamaica 1965/66. MCC to Australia and New Zealand 1962/63; Commonwealth to India 1964/65. Played in 7 test matches, 1962 to 1964. Highest test score: 6* v Australia, Lord's 1964. Best test bowling: 6–85 v Pakistan, Lord's 1962 (on Test debut). Test record: 9 runs (4.50); 22 wickets (27.72). Full first-class record; 1474 runs (5.94); 1076 wickets (21.18). Played Devon, 1952–53.

COLLIER, Christopher George Arthur – RHB RAS
b. Banff, Scotland, 23 August 1886; d. in action, Mametz, France, 25 August 1916.
   Debut 1910 v War., Worcester 1910. 52 matches for W 1910–14 (professional). Highest score: W 72 v Hants, Portsmouth 1912. Best bowling: W 3–51 v Oxford U, Oxford 1911. Best first-class bowling, 3–28, H.K. Foster's team v Oxford U, Oxford 1912.

COLLINSON, John – RHB OB
b. Sotterley, Suffolk, 2 October 1911; d. Hove, Sussex, 29 August 1979.

Educated at St John's School, Leatherhead.

Debut 1946 v Combined Services, Worcester. 1 match for W 1946 (amateur). Scored 23 and 1 only match.

2 matches for Middx. 1939. Highest first-class score 34, Middx. v Glos., Cheltenham 1939.

CONWAY, Arthur Joseph – RHB RFM

b. Stirchley, Birmingham, 1 April 1885; d. Blackpool, 29 October 1954.

Debut 1910 v Hants, Worcester. 29 matches for W 1910–19 (professional). Highest score: W 20* v Oxford U, Oxford 1911. Best bowling: W 9–38 v Glos, Moreton-in-Marsh, 1914.

Birmingham League for Kidderminster.

Played Soccer for Wolverhampton Wanderers.

COOPER, Edwin – RHB

b. Bacup, Lancs, 30 November 1915; d. Birmingham, 29 October 1968.

Debut 1936 v Oxford U, Oxford. 249 matches for W (professional) 1936–51. Cap 1937; benefit (£3,000) 1951.

Highest score: W 216* v War., Dudley 1938. 1000 runs (9) – 1916 (43.54) 1949 best. Carried bat throughout innings twice; 104*/273 v Lancs., Old Trafford 1939; 69*/154 v War., Dudley 1951. 191 and 106* in match v Northants, Kidderminster 1946.

Birmingham League for Aston Unity. Played Devon 1953–54 while coach at RNC, Dartmouth. Coach, Bedford School 1958–68.

Brother Fred Cooper (W).

E. Cooper

A.J. Conway

C.F. Corden

F. Cooper

COOPER, Fred – RHB
b. Bacup, Lancs., 18 April 1921; d. Stourbridge, 22 December 1986.
Debut 1947 v S. Africa, Worcester 1947. 40 matches W 1947–50 (professional). Highest score: W 113* v Notts., Trent Bridge 1948.
4 matches for Lancs, 1946. Birmingham League cricket for Old Hill, Kidderminster.
Brother Edwin Cooper (W).

CORBETT, Percival Thomas – RHB
b. Fernhill Heath, North Claines, nr Ombersley, 20 February 1900; d. West Malvern, 26 June 1944.
Debut 1922 v Kent, Kidderminster. 7 matches for W (professional) 1922–23. Highest score: W 20 on debut above.
Became professional at Liverpool and latterly a publican at West Malvern.

CORDEN, Charles Frederic – RHB
b. Croydon, Surrey, 30 December 1874; d. Croydon, 26 February 1924.
Debut 1900 v London County, Worcester. 17 matches for W (professional) 1900–03. Highest score: W 64 v Sussex, Hove 1902.
Played for Mitcham CC.

COVENTRY, Hon. John Bonynge – RHB SLA

b. London, 9 January 1903; d. Pirton, W, 4 July 1969. Educated at Eton and Magdalen College, Oxford U.

Debut 1919 v H.K. Foster's XI, Worcester. 75 matches for W 1919–35 (amateur). W captain 1929–30. Highest score: W 86 v Derby., Worcester 1922. Best bowling: W 2–18 v H.K. Foster's XI, Worcester 1919 (debut).

Uncles: Hon. C.J. Coventry (England) and Hon. H.T. Coventry (MCC).

COX, Gilbert Clifford – RHB

b. Stroud, Glos., 5 July 1908; d. Alcester, War. 31 March 1974. Educated at Worcester Royal Grammar School.

Debut 1935 v Lancs., Kidderminster. 2 matches for W 1935 (amateur). Highest score: W 19 on debut.

CRAWLEY, Leonard George – RHB RFM

b. Nacton, Suffolk, 26 July 1903; d. Worlington, Suffolk, 9 July 1981. Educated at Harrow and Pembroke College, Cambridge U.

Debut 1922 v Som., Weston-super-Mare. 6 matches for W 1922–23 (amateur). Highest score: W 161 v Northants, Worcester 1923.

34 matches Cambridge U 1923–25; Blue each season. 56 matches Essex

J.B. Coventry

L.G. Crawley

R.J. Crisp

1926–36. Tour; MCC to W. Indies 1925/26. Highest first-class score: 222, Essex v Glam., Swansea 1928. First-class career record; 5227 runs (31.11).

Good amateur golfer, appearing in the British Walker Cup team, and well known golf writer. Brother C.L. Crawley (Essex).

CRISP, Robert James – RHB RF
b. Calcutta, India, 28 May 1911.

Debut 1938 v Australia, Worcester. 8 matches for W 1938 (amateur). Highest score: W 29 v Som., Taunton 1938. Best bowling: W 7–82 v Middx., Lord's 1938.

Played Rhodesia 1929/30–1930/31; Western Province 1931/32–1935/36. Toured England with S. Africa 1935; toured Ceylon with Sir Julien Cahn 1936/37. 9 tests for S. Africa 1935–1935/36. Highest first-class score 45, S. Africa v Hants, Southampton 1935. Best first-class bowling: 9–64, Western Province v Natal, Durban 1933/34. Twice took 4 wickets in 4 balls – unique in first-class cricket – Western Province v Griqualand West, Jo'burg 1931/32, and Western Province v Natal, Durban 1933/34. Also took 4 wickets in 5 balls (and hat trick) Western Province v Transvaal, Jo'burg 1931/32. Highest test score: 35 v Australia, Durban 1935/36. Best test bowling: 5–99 v England, Old Trafford 1935.

Latterly became schoolmaster and proprietor in England, and journalist in England and S. Africa, before living 'Bohemian' life on Greek island.

CROWE, George Lawson – RHB

b. Worcester, 8 January 1885; d. Bromley, Kent, 23 June 1976. Educated at Tonbridge and Westminster schools.

Debut 1906 v Hants, Stourbridge scoring 78 and 37. 23 matches for W (amateur) 1906–13. Highest score: W 78 on debut above.

Played Bickley Cricket Club. For many years master at Bromley Grammar School, Kent.

CUFFE, John Alexander – RHB SLA

b. Toowoomba, Queensland, Australia, 26 June 1880; d. 16 May 1931 – found drowned at Burton-on-Trent, Staffs.

Debut 1903 v Oxford U, Oxford. 215 matches for W (professional) 1903–14. Highest score: W 145 v Hants, Bournemouth 1905. Best bowling: W 9–38 v Yorks., Bradford 1907. 1000 runs (3) – 1112 (31.77) 1906 best. 100 wickets (2) – 110 (23.56) 1911 best. 'Double' in 1911 – 1054 runs (25.70): 110 wickets (23.56). Hat trick v Hants, Bournemouth 1910.

1 match for New South Wales 1920/03.

First-class umpire 1925–27. Appointed coach at Repton School shortly before death. Played soccer for Glossop.

CUMBES, James – RHB RFM

b. East Didsbury, Manchester, 4 May 1944. Educated at Didsbury Technical High School.

J.A. Cuffe

G.L. Crowe

J. Cumbes

T.S. Curtis

Debut 1972 v Glam., Cardiff. 109 matches for W 1972–81; cap 1978. Highest score: W 43 v Sussex, Hove 1980. Best bowling: W 6–24 v Yorks., Worcester 1977.

9 matches Lancs 1963–71; 29 matches Surrey 1968–69. 14 matches War., 1982. Commercial manager War. 1982–86. Joined Lancs. in similar post 1987. 379 wickets (30.20) in first-class cricket. Birmingham League for West Bromwich Dartmouth.

Retired from playing 1982 due to illness. Soccer (goalkeeper) for Tranmere Rovers, West Bromwich Albion, Aston Villa.

CURTIS, Timothy Stephen – RHB LB
b. Chislehurst, Kent, 15 January 1960. Educated at Worcester Royal Grammar School; Durham University; Magdalene College, Cambridge U.

Debut 1979 v Sri Lanka, Worcester. 161 matches for W 1979–date. Highest score: W 156 v Essex, Colchester 1989. Best bowling: W 2–72 v War., Worcester 1987. 1000 runs (6) – 1601 (37.08) 1987 best.

5 tests for England 1988–89; 140 runs (15.55). Highest test score: 41 v Australia, 1989. 10 matches for Cambridge U 1983, winning Blue. Holds

W 2nd wicket record – 287* with G.A. Hick v Glam., Neath 1986. Birmingham League cricket for West Bromwich Dartmouth and Kidderminster.

A group of happy and thoughtful cricketers.
Back: Holder, Headley
Front: Basil D'Oliveria, Wilcox, Brain and Gifford

D

DARKS, Geoffrey Charlton – RHB RMF
b. Bewdley, 28 June 1926. Educated at New Meeting School, Kidderminster.

Debut 1946 v Leics., Ashby-de-la-Zouch. 7 matches for W (professional) 1946–50. Highest score: W 39 v Cambridge U, Worcester 1950. Best bowling: W 5–49 v Combined Services, Worcester 1950.

Birmingham League cricket for Kidderminster; club cricket for Whitehaven, Carpet Trades, Smethwick Drop Forgings.

DAVIDGE, Guy Mortimer Coleridge – RHB
b. Woolwich, Kent, 2 March 1878; d. Hove, 17 February 1956. Educated at Newton College.

Debut 1911 v Oxford U, Oxford. 1 match for W 1911 (amateur). 0 runs in only innings.

Regular Army Officer (Captain).

G.C. Darks

T.E. Davies

J.P. Davis

DAVIES, Trefor Elliot – RHB LB
b. Stourbridge, 14 March 1938.
 Debut 1955 v Oxford U, Oxford. 20 matches for W (professional) 1955–61. Highest score: W 76 v Glam., Cardiff 1961. Best bowling: W 2–22 v Cambridge U, Worcester 1955.
 Birmingham League Cricket for Stourbridge.

DAVIS, John Percy – RHB
b. Lye, 26 January 1884; d. Stourbridge, 16 February 1951.
 Debut 1922 v War., Stourbridge. 4 matches for W (amateur) 1922. Highest score: W 38* v War., Stourbridge on debut.
 Birmingham League cricket for Stourbridge.
 Brother Major Davis (W).

DAVIS, Major – RHB WK
b. Lye, 27 March 1882; d. Kidderminster, 27 April 1959.
 Debut 1911 v Oxford U, Oxford. 1 match for W (amateur) 1911.

Scored 29 and 6 in only match.
  Birmingham League cricket for Stourbridge.
  Brother J.P. Davis (W).

DAYS, John Edward ('Ben') –
b. Peopleton, near Upton Snodsbury, 10 July 1872. d. Walsall, Staffs., 1947.
  Debut 1900 v War., Edgbaston. 2 matches for W (professional) 1900–07. Highest score: W 5 v Surrey, The Oval 1907. Best bowling: W 2–42 v War., Edgbaston 1900.
  Played Staffs. in Minor Counties Championship 1910–14. Played Astwood Bank CC.

DEVEREUX, Louis Norman – RHB OB
b. Heavitree, Exeter, Devon, 20 October 1931.
  Debut 1950 v Cambridge U, Worcester. 79 matches for W (professional) 1950–55. Highest score: W 81* v War., Worcester 1953. Best bowling: W 4–103 v Som., Worcester 1952.
  2 matches Middx, 1949; 106 matches Glam. (and cap 1956) 1956–60. Highest first-class score: 108*, Glam. v Lancs., Old Trafford 1957. Best first-class bowling: 6–29 Glam. v Yorks., Middlesbrough 1956. Scored 1039 runs (22.58) in 1957. 5560 runs (19.86) and 178 wickets (35.32) in first-class cricket. Played for Gorseinon in S. Wales.
  English table tennis International in 1949.

L.N. Devereux

G. Dews

R.J. Devereux

DEVEREUX, Richard Jeynes – RHB LM
b. Castle Bromwich, War., 26 December 1938. Educated at Malvern.
Debut 1963 v Middx., Lord's. 11 matches for W 1963. Highest score: W 55* v Cambridge U, Worcester 1963. Best bowling: W 3–44 in same match.
Birmingham League cricket for Walsall, Moseley and West Bromwich Dartmouth.

DEWS, George – RHB
b. Ossett, Yorks., 5 June 1921.
Debut 1946 v Lancs., Old Trafford. 374 matches for W (professional) 1946–61. Cap 1950; benefit (£2,795) 1960. Highest score: W 145 v Combined Services, Worcester 1951. 1000 runs (11) – 1752 (41.71) 1959 best. Dismissed first ball in each innings on debut.
Birmingham League for Dudley.
Played soccer for Middlesbrough, Plymouth Argyle and Walsall.

DILLEY, Graham Roy – LHB RFM
b. Dartford, Kent, 18 May 1959. Educated at Dartford West Secondary School.

Debut 1987 v Kent, Worcester. 29 matches for W 1987–date (cap 1987). Highest score: W 36 v Glos., Bristol 1988. Best bowling: W 6–43 v Leics., Worcester 1987.

41 tests for England 1979–89. Highest test score: 56 v Australia, Headingley 1981. Best test bowling: 6–38 v New Zealand, Christchurch 1987/88. 521 test runs (13.35); 138 test wickets (29.67). 198 matches Kent 1977–86 (cap 1980). Played Natal in Currie Cup 1985/86. Highest first-class score: 81, Kent v Northants, Northampton 1979. Best first-class bowling 7–63, Natal v Transvaal, Johannesburg 1985/86. First class career record: 2056 runs (13.98); 587 wickets (26.68).

D'OLIVEIRA, Basil Lewis – RHB RFM/M
b. Signal Hill, Cape Town, S. Africa, 4 October 1931. Educated at Zonnebloem College, Cape Town.

Debut 1964 v Australia, Worcester. 275 matches for W 1964–80. Cap 1965; benefit (£27,000) 1975. Highest score: W 227 v Yorks., Hull 1974. Best bowling: W 6–29 v Hants, Portsmouth 1968. 1000 runs (6) – 1653 (44.67) 1965 best.

First-class debut, Commonwealth XI v Rhodesia 1961/62. 44 test

B.L. D'Oliveira

G.R. Dilley

D.B. D'Oliveria

matches for England, 1966–72. Highest test score: 158 v Australia, The
Oval 1968. Best test bowling: 3–46 v Pakistan, Headingley 1971. Test
tours to W. Indies 1967/68, Pakistan 1968/69, New Zealand 1970/71 and
Australia 1970/71. Selected for England tour of S. Africa 1968/69; refusal
of S. African government to accept the selection led to a break off of
cricketing relations between the two countries. Also toured with W to
Rhodesia 1964/65 and Jamaica 1965/66, and undertook various tours with
Commonwealth and International teams, 1961/62 to 1972/73. Test career
record; 2484 runs (40.06); 47 wickets (39.53). First-class career record;
18918 runs (39.57); 548 wickets (27.41). Played Birmingham League
cricket for Kidderminster.

Worcs coach since 1980. Awarded OBE in 1969. Son D.B. D'Oliveira
(W).

D'OLIVEIRA, Damian Basil – RHB RM/OB
b. Cape Town, S. Africa, 19 October 1960. Educated at Blessed Edward
Oldcorne Secondary School, Worcester.

Debut 1982 v Zimbabwe, Worcester 1982. 157 matches for W 1982–89.
Cap 1985. Highest score: W 146* v Glos., Bristol 1986. Best bowling:
2–17 v Glos., Bristol 1986. 1000 runs (3) – 1244 (29.61) 1985 best.

Birmingham League cricket for Worcester City.

Father B.L. D'Oliveira (W and England); uncle I.D'Oliveira (Leics.).

DORRELL, Philip George – RHB
b. Worcester, 6 December 1914. Educated at Bromsgrove and Brasenose College, Oxford U.

Debut 1946 v Northants, Northampton. 1 match for W 1946 (amateur). Scored 1 in only innings.

Played Worcester City.

DUFF, Alan Robert – RHB LBG
b. Kinver, Staffs., 12 January 1938; d. Malvern, 28 June 1989. Educated at Radley and Lincoln College, Oxford U.

Debut 1960 v Sussex, Worcester 1961 (amateur). 6 matches for W 1960–61. Highest score: W 50* v Notts., Trent Bridge 1960. Best bowling: W 4–24 v Notts., Trent Bridge 1960.

24 matches Oxford U, 1959–61 (Blue 1960, 1961). Highest first-class score: 55*, Oxford v War., Oxford 1959. First-class career record; 676 runs (16.49); 54 wickets (25.85).

Assistant manager, England Youth to W. Indies 1972/73.

A.R. Duff

P.G. Dorrell

EDEN, Ernest – B RFM
b. Blockley, nr Moreton-in-Marsh, Glos.
   Debut 1923 v Derbys., Dudley. 1 match for W (professional) 1923.
Scored 9 and 18* in only match.
   1 match for Glos. 1921. Birmingham League cricket for Smethwick;
also played Witham CC (Essex).
   Soccer (full-back) for Walsall.

EDWARDS, Herbert Charles – RHB LB
b. Colley Gate, nr Halesowen, 3 December 1913.
   Debut 1946 v Lancs., Old Trafford. 1 match for W 1946 (amateur).
Scored 10 and 1 in only innings.
   Birmingham League for Old Hill.

E. Eden

J.W. Elliott

R.M. Ellcock

ELLCOCK, Ricardo McDonald – RHB RFM
b. Bridgetown, Barbados, 17 June 1965. Educated at Malvern College.

Debut 1982 v Middlesex, Worcester. 29 matches for W 1982–88. Highest score: W 45* v Essex, Worcester 1984. Best bowling: W 4–34 v Glam., Worcester 1984.

Played for Barbados 1983/84. Played 8 matches for Middx 1989, and won selection for England tour of West Indies. Best first-class bowling: 5–35 Middx v Yorks., Headingley 1989. Birmingham League cricket, Worcester City and West Bromwich Dartmouth.

Troubled by back injury while with W.

ELLIOTT, John William – LHB WK
b. Worcester, 12 February 1942. Educated at Worcester Royal Grammar School.

Debut 1959 v Som., Worcester. 10 matches for W 1959–65 (started as amateur). Highest score: 18* v Oxford U, Oxford 1961. Subsequently on W committee.

Birmingham League for Kidderminster and Walsall.

P.S. Evans

EVANS, Percy Stanbrook – B SLA
b. China c 1900.

Debut 1928 v Glam., Cardiff. 5 matches for W (amateur) 1928. Highest score: W 5 v Glam., Cardiff (on debut). Best bowling: W 3–84 v Glam., Cardiff 1928 (on debut).

Son of a medical missionary and member of a Worcester family, he was brought up in the Far East.

EVANS, William Henry Brereton – RHB RFM
b. in S. Africa, 29 January 1883; d. in a flying accident at Farnborough, Hants, 7 August 1913. Educated at Malvern.

Debut 1901 v Sussex, Worcester. 6 matches for W 1901 (amateur). Highest score: W 107 v Glos., Worcester 1901. Best bowling: W 1–21 v Derby., Derby 1906.

Played for Hants 20 matches 1902–10. Oxford U, 31 matches 1902–05. Blue all four seasons. Highest first-class score: 142 Oxford U v Sussex, Hove. Best first-class bowling: 7–41 Oxford U v Somerset. Oxford 1903. Soccer Blue at Oxford.

Brothers A.E. and D.M. Evans (both Hants).

EVERITT, Russell Stanley – RHB
b. King's Heath, Birmingham, 8 September 1881; d. Kew Gardens, Surrey, 11 May 1973. Educated at Malvern.

Debut 1901 v Cambridge U, Cambridge. 1 match for W (amateur) 1901. Scored 6* and 0 in only match. 3 matches for War. 1909. Highest first-class score: 38. War. v Surrey, The Oval 1909.

Birmingham League cricket for Moseley. Other cricket for Olton and Richmond (Surrey).

EVERS, Ralph Denis Mark – RHB
b. Stourbridge, 11 August 1913. Educated at Haileybury and ISC.
Debut 1936 v Northants, Kettering. 15 matches for W 1936–38
(amateur). Highest score: 60* v Notts., Worcester 1938.
Birmingham League cricket for Stourbridge.

R.D.M. Evers

FARNFIELD, Percy Hamilton – RHB
b. Guildford, Surrey, 16 June 1881. d. Solihull, War. 19 August 1962.
Debut 1925 v Hants, Worcester. 1 match for W (amateur) 1925. Failed to score in only innings.

FAWCUS, Charles Leslie Dinsdale – LHB LM
b. Bromley, Kent, 8 December 1898; d. Sussex, 8 December 1967. Educated at Bradfield and Christ Church College, Oxford U.
Debut 1925 v Oxford U, Oxford. 1 match for W (amateur) 1925. Highest score: W 43 in first innings of debut match.
1 match for Kent in 1924; 5 matches for Oxford U 1925–26. Highest first-class score: 70, Oxford U v Surrey, The Oval 1926. Played Dorset in Minor Counties Championship 1933 and 34.

C.D. Fearnley

J. FEREDAY.

C.A.F. Fiddian-Green

FEARNLEY, Charles 'Duncan' – LHB
b. Pudsey, Yorks., 12 April 1940.

Debut 1962 v Glam., Worcester. 97 matches for W. 1962–68, starting as a professional. Highest score: W 112 v Derby., Kidderminster 1966. Currently W CCC Chairman.

Played for Lincs. in Minor Counties 1969–71. Birmingham League cricket for West Bromwich Dartmouth. Yorkshire club cricket for Farsley.

Is a well-known manufacturer of cricket bats, and retailer of cricket equipment. Brother M.C. Fearnley played Yorks.

FEREDAY, John Benjamin – RHB OB
b. Burnt Tree, Dudley, 24 November 1873; d. Holy Cross, 1 January 1958.

Debut 1899 v MCC, Lord's. 10 matches for W 1899–1901 (professional). Highest score: W 37 v S. Africa, Worcester 1901. Best bowling: W 1–27 v Yorks., Worcester 1900.

Birmingham League professional for Mitchells & Butlers and Handsworth Wood. Played Staffordshire in Minor Counties Championship 1902–11.

Father Alfred Fereday played Dudley and well-known umpire in Midland cricket.

FIDDIAN-GREEN, Charles Anderson Fiddian – RHB RM
b. Handsworth, Birmingham, 22 December 1898; d. Malvern, 5 September 1976. Educated at The Leys School & Jesus College, Cambridge U.

Debut 1931 v Essex, Worcester. 24 matches for W (amateur) 1931–34. Highest score: W 108 v Essex, Worcester (debut).

17 matches for Cambridge U 1921–22 (Blue each season). 4350 runs (31.07) in all first-class cricket.

Played hockey, Cambridge U and England.

FIELD, Frank – RHB RFM

b. Langley, W, 29 February 1908; d. Stourbridge, 25 April 1981.

Debut 1928 v Notts., Dudley. 2 matches for W 1928–31 (professional). Highest score: W 12 v Notts., Worcester 1931. Best bowling: W 4–60 v Notts., Dudley 1928 (on debut).

FISHER, Paul Bernard – RHB WK

b. Edmonton, London, 19 December 1954. Educated at St Ignatius College, Enfield and Christ Church College, Oxford U.

Debut 1980 v Glos., Cheltenham. 14 matches W 1980–81. Highest score: W 28* v Surrey, The Oval 1981.

2 matches for Middx., 1979. 41 matches for Oxford U 1974–78 (Blue 1975–78). Played Birmingham League for Dudley.

·FLAVELL, John Alfred – LHB RFM

b. Brierley Hill, Staffs., 15 May 1929. Educated at Kingswinford Secondary School.

Debut 1949 v Essex, Southend. 392 matches for W 1949–67. Cap 1955; benefit (£6,840) 1963. Highest score: W 54 v War., Dudley 1959. Best bowling: W 9–30 v Kent, Dover 1955. Three hat tricks in career – all for W: v Kent, Kidderminster 1951; v Cambridge, Cambridge 1953; v Lancs., Old Trafford 1963 (all lbw). Apart from best bowling above, took 9–56, W v Middx., Kidderminster 1964; 9–122 W v Sussex, Hastings 1954.

4 tests for England 1961–64; took 7 wickets (52.42). Full first-class

J.A. Flavell

P.B. Fisher

B.S. Foster

C.K. Foster

career record: 2032 runs (6.51); 1529 wickets (21.48). 100 wickets W 8 times; 158 (17.21) 1961 best. Birmingham League cricket for Stourbridge & Walsall.

Played pro-League soccer for Walsall.

FOLEY, Henry 'Thomas' Hamilton – LHB

b. Hereford, 25 April 1905; d. Stoke Edith, Hereford, 13 December 1959. Educated at Eton.

Debut 1925 v Oxford U, Oxford. 1 match for W (amateur) 1925. 6 and 0* in only match.

FOSTER, Basil Samuel – RHB

b. Malvern, 12 February 1882; d. Hillingdon, Middx., 28 September 1959. Educated at Malvern.

Debut 1902 v Kent, Tonbridge. 7 matches for W (amateur) 1902–11. Highest score: W 36 v Middx., Lord's 1911.

Played 12 matches Middx. 1912; also played MCC. 753 runs (14.76) in first-class career.

Enjoyed career as actor and theatre manager.

FOSTER, Christopher Knollys – RHB

b. Ledbury, 27 September 1904; d. Kingsthorne, Hereford, 4 December 1971. Educated at Malvern.

Debut 1927 v Middx., Worcester 1927. 3 matches for W (amateur) 1927. Highest score: W 16* v New Zealand, Worcester 1927.

Father H.K. Foster (W).

G.N. Foster

H.K. Foster

FOSTER, Geoffrey Norman – RHB

b. Malvern, 16 October 1884; d. Westminster, London, 11 August 1971.
Educated at Malvern and Worcester College, Oxford U.

Debut 1911 v Leics., Worcester. 81 matches for W 1903–14 (amateur).
Highest score: W 175 v Leics., Leicester 1913. Best bowling: W 2–21 v
War., Worcester 1908.

26 matches for Oxford U 1905–08 (Blue each season). 10 matches for
Kent 1921–22. 6600 runs (28.32) in first-class career, with 11 centuries.

Represented England Amateurs at Soccer. One of Foster
'Brotherhood'. Son P.G. Foster (Kent). Son-in-law F.G.H. Chalk
(Kent).

FOSTER, Henry Knollys – RHB RFM

b. Malvern, 30 October 1873; d. Kingsthorne, Hereford, 23 June 1950.

Educated at Malvern and Trinity College, Oxford U. Debut 1899 v
Yorks., Worcester. 246 matches for W 1899–1925 (amateur). Captain
1901–1910; 1913. Highest score: W 216 v Som., Worcester 1903. (Also
scored 215 v War., Worcester 1908.) Best bowling: W 2–16 v Derby.,
Worcester 1899. Added 309 for 1st wicket with F.L. Bowley, W v
Derby., Derby 1901, the 1st wicket record for the county. 1000 runs (7) –
1596 (42.00) 1903 best.

Was a top-line racquets player. A member of the Foster brotherhood.

FOSTER, Maurice Kirshaw – RHB RMF
b. Malvern, 1 January 1889; d. Lichfield, Staffs., 3 December 1940. Educated at Malvern.

Debut 1908 v Yorks., Sheffield. 157 matches for W (amateur) 1908–34. Captain 1923–25. Highest score: W 158 v Derby., Worcester 1914. Best bowling: W 2–17 v Surrey, Worcester 1909. 1000 runs (5) 1480 (32.88) 1927 best. Scored 141 and 106, W v Hants, Worcester 1926. 8295 runs (28.70) with 12 centuries in all first-class cricket.

Birmingham League cricket for West Bromwich Dartmouth and Walsall.

FOSTER, Neville John Acland – RHB
b. Malvern, 28 September 1890; d. Malvern, 8 January 1978. Educated at Malvern.

Debut 1914 v Middx., Lord's. 8 matches for W 1914–23 (amateur). Highest score: W 40* v Derby., Derby 1923.

Played cricket in Malaya and skippered Federated Malay States side.

Member of Foster brotherhood.

N.J.A. Foster

M.K. Foster

R.E. Foster   *W.L. Foster*

FOSTER, Reginald Erskine – RHB RFM

b. Malvern, 16 April 1878; d. Kensington, London, 13 May 1914.
Educated at Malvern and University College, Oxford.

Debut 1899 v Yorks., Worcester. 80 matches for W (amateur) 1899–1912. (Captain 1901). Highest score: W 246* v Kent, Worcester 1905. Scored 134* and 101, W v Hants, Worcester 1899. (Brother W.L. Foster also scored two centuries – the first time this had been done twice in the same innings.) 1996 runs (51.17) in 1901. Best bowling: W 3–54 v Glos., Worcester 1900.

31 matches for Oxford U 1897–1900 (Blue each season); Captain 1900. 8 tests for England 1903/04–1907 (Capt – 3 – in 1907). Highest score 287 v Australia, Sydney 1903/04 on debut. This remains the highest score on test debut and the highest for England in Australia. 602 runs (46.30) in tests. 9076 runs (41.82) with 22 centuries in all first-class cricket. Obtained century before lunch on six occasions, 4 for W. Birmingham League cricket for Stourbridge.

Captained England at soccer.

FOSTER, Wilfred Lionel – RHB

b. Malvern, 2 December 1874; d. Shifnal, Shrops. 22 March 1958.
Educated at Malvern.

Debut 1899 v Yorks., Worcester. 29 matches for W (amateur) 1899–1911. Highest score: W 172* v Hants, Worcester 1899; scored 140

The Foster Family
Back row: R.E., Rev Foster, B.S.
Middle: W.L., H.K.
Front: M.K., N.J.A., G.N.

J. Fox

W.V. Fox

in first innings – with brother R.E. Foster achieved first instance of two batsmen scoring two centuries in same match for same side.

An army officer, his duties limited his appearances. Top-class soccer player. Member of Foster brotherhood.

FOWLER, Richard Harold – RHB RFM
b. Islington, London, 5 March 1887; d. Clent, 27 October 1970.

Debut 1921 v War., Worcester. 4 matches for W (amateur) 1921. Highest score: 34 v War., Worcester 1921 on debut. Best bowling: 5–33 v Glos., Stourbridge 1921.

Was a clerk in Holy Orders. His bowling action was so doubtful that he was informed only his 'calling' saved him from being no-balled.

FOX, John – LHB SLA
b. Selly Park, Birmingham, 7 September 1904; d. Birmingham, 15 November 1961.

Debut 1929 v S. Africa, Worcester. 94 matches for W 1929–33 (professional). Highest score: W 73 v Northants, Worcester 1931. Best bowling: W 4–77 v Glos., Worcester 1930. Best first-class bowling 4–27, War. v W, Edgbaston 1926.

FOX, William Victor – RHB
b. Middlesbrough, Yorks, 8 January 1898; d. Withington, Manchester, 17 February 1949.

Debut 1923 v Hants, Southampton. 163 matches for W 1923–32 (professional). Highest score: W 198 v War., Edgbaston 1929. 1000 runs (3) – 1457 (31.00) 1929 best. Played regularly 1923 but then was adjudged not to be qualified and did not play again until 1926.

Birmingham League cricket for Dudley.

Professional soccer for Middlesbrough, Wolves and Newport County.

FRANCIS, Percy Thomas – RHB
b. Ash, Walsham-le-Willows, Suffolk, 6 May 1875; d. Branksome, Poole, Dorset, 8 September 1964.
   Debut 1901 v Cambridge U, Cambridge. 3 matches for W (amateur) 1901–02. Highest score: W 66 v Cambridge U, Cambridge 1901 on debut.
   Played Suffolk in Minor Counties Championship 1904–05.

FULTON, Herbert Angus – WK
b. Bangalore, India, 3 October 1872; d. Minehead, Som., 23 December 1951.
   Debut 1914 v Leics., Worcester 1914. 1 match for W (amateur) 1914. 2* in only innings.
   A major in the Army who deputized for E.W. Bale.

Worcestershire's debut in first-class cricket, 1899. Back row (l to r): G.F. Wheldon, G.A. Wilson, P.H. Foley (secretary), E.G. Arnold, R.D. Burrows. Middle row: W.L. Foster, E.G. Bromley-Martin, H.K. Foster (capt.), R.E. Foster, G.E. Bromley-Martin. Front: T. Straw and A. Bird.

GALE, Leslie Edward – RHB RAS

b. Solihull, War., 11 November 1904; d. Dudley, 22 January 1982.

Debut 1923 v War., Edgbaston. 14 matches for W (amateur) 1923–28. Highest score: W 19 v Northants, Worcester 1923. Best bowling: 5–49 v War., Edgbaston 1923 (on debut).

Birmingham League cricket for Dudley.

GARRATT, Humphrey Stone – B WK

b. Kingston-upon-Thames, Surrey, 12 January 1898; d. Worplesden, Surrey, 1 September 1974. Educated at Haileybury.

Debut 1925 v Oxford U., Oxford. 5 matches for W (amateur) 1925–28. Highest score W 39 v Yorks., Worcester 1928.

Regular Army officer, which precluded regular appearances.

L.E. Gale

G.W. Gaukrodger

GAUKRODGER, George Warrington – RHB WK
b. Leeds, 11 September 1877; d. Low Moor, Bradford, 4 January 1938.
    Debut 1900 v London County, Worcester. 115 matches for W
(professional) 1900–10. Highest score: W 91 v Lancs., Liverpool 1903.
Dismissed 6 batsmen (4 ct 2 st) in innings, W v Kent, Tunbridge Wells,
1907; this was the county record at the time and has still only been
equalled in County Championship matches.
    Professional in Bradford League after retirement from county cricket.

GENDERS, William 'Roy' – RHB Occasional bowler
b. Dore, Derby., 21 January 1913; d. Worthing, Sussex, 28 September
1985. Educated at King's School, Ely; St John's College, Cambridge U.
    Debut 1947 v Derby., Chesterfield. 5 matches for W (amateur)
1947–48. Highest score: W 55* v Derby., Chesterfield 1947 (on debut).
Best bowling: W 2–43 v Glos., Worcester 1947.
    3 matches for Derby. 1946; 2 matches for Som. 1949. Birmingham
League cricket for Smethwick.
    A journalist: wrote *League Cricket in England* and *Worcestershire
County Cricket*, both published 1952.

W.G. Gethin

S.J. Gethin

GETHIN, Stanley John – RHB RM
b. Kidderminster, 16 February 1875; d. Kidderminster, 17 February 1950.
   Debut 1900 v Yorks., Bradford. 4 matches for W 1900–01 (amateur). Highest score: W 41 v Leics., Leicester 1900. Best bowling: W 1–25 v London County, Worcester 1900.
   Birmingham League cricket for Kidderminster.
   Brother W.G. Gethin (W).

GETHIN, William George – RHB RM
b. Kidderminster, 4 May 1877; d. Kidderminster, 4 November 1939.
   Debut 1921 v Glam., Kidderminster. 1 match for W (amateur) 1921. Scored 19 and 1 in only match.
   Birmingham League cricket for Kidderminster.
   Brother S.J. Gethin (W).

H.H.I.H. Gibbons

GIBBONS, Harry Harold Ian Haywood ('Doc') – RHB Occasional RAB
b. Devonport, Devon, 8 October 1904; d. Worcester, 16 February 1973.
Educated at Kilburn Grammar School.

Debut 1927 v New Zealand, Worcester. 380 matches for W
(professional until 1939; amateur thereafter) 1927–46. Cap 1928; benefit
1938. Highest score: W 212* v Northants, Dudley 1939. Best bowling: W
2–27 v New Zealand, Worcester 1927 (on debut). 1000 runs (12) – 2654
(52.03) 1934 best (the county record). Scored 200* v W. Indies,
Worcester 1928 – a W record against any Tourists. Carried bat
throughout an innings twice – 70*/165 v War., Kidderminster 1934;
83*/148 v Lancs., Kidderminster 1935. Scored 111* and 100* v Hants,
Worcester 1939 – the only case of unbeaten centuries in each innings for
W. Apart from county record above, also scored 2120 runs (43.26) in
1938 and 2008 runs (37.88) in 1933. Added 274 for 2nd wicket with
Nawab of Pataudi v Kent, Worcester 1933, added 277 for 4th wicket with
B.W. Quaife v Middx., Worcester 1931; added 197 for 7th wicket with R.
Howorth v Surrey, the Oval 1938. All these were W records at the time.
Scored centuries before Lunch v Hants, Southampton, and v Kent,
Worcester in 1928. These were his first centuries in first-class cricket and
he achieved a unique feat in first-class cricket with his pre-Lunch
hundreds.

Birmingham League cricket for Dudley; also played for Hampstead
(London).

Norman Gifford, Basil D'Oliveira and Alan Ormrod take a 'raincheck'

H.A. Gilbert

GIFFORD, Norman – LHB SLA
b. Ulverston, Lancs., 30 March 1940; Educated at Ulverston Secondary School.

Debut 1960 v Kent, Tunbridge Wells. 521 matches for W 1960–82 (initially as professional). Cap 1961; benefit (£11,047) 1974; testimonial 1981. County captain 1971–80. Highest score: W 89 v Oxford U, Oxford 1963. Best bowling: W 8–28 v Yorks., Sheffield 1968. 100 wickets (3) – 133 (19.66) 1961 best. Achieved hat trick v Derby., Chesterfield 1965. Match figures of 14–76 v Cambridge U, Cambridge 1972.

Played 139 matches for War. 1983–88; cap 1983, captain 1985–87. 15 tests for England 1964–73; 33 wickets (31.09); best test bowling analysis 5–55 v Pakistan, Karachi 1972/73. *Wisden* Cricketer of Year 1974; awarded MBE for cricket services 1982. Test selector 1982; appointed cricket manager to Sussex CCC 1989. First-class record: 7047 runs (13.02); 2068 wickets (23.56). Birmingham League cricket for Dudley.

GILBERT, Humphrey Adam ('Barmy') – RHB RM/OB
b. Bombay, India, 2 June 1886; d. Bishopstone, Hereford, 19 July 1960. Educated at Charterhouse and Christ Church College, Oxford U.

Debut 1921 v War., Worcester. 72 matches for W 1921–30 (amateur). Highest score: W 31* v Derby., Kidderminster 1928. Best bowling: W 7–60 (13–116 match) v Notts., Worcester 1921.

24 matches for Oxford 1907–09 (Blue each season). Highest first-class score 35* Oxford U v Surrey, The Oval 1908. Best first-class bowling 8–48 Oxford U v MCC, Oxford 1907. Minor Counties Championship for Monmouth 1913.

W.A. Goodreds

GOOD, Dennis Cunliffe – RHB RFM
b. Leeds, 29 August 1926. Educated at Denstone, Sheffield U.
Debut 1946 v Combined Services, Worcester 1946. 1 match for W (professional) 1946. Scored 1 and 6*; 1 wicket for 75.
3 matches for Glam. 1947. Highest first-class score 21, Glam. v Derby., Derby 1947. Best first-class bowling 2–34 same match. Played for RAF and for Rawdon CC (Yorks).

GOODREDS, William Arthur – RHB RFM
b. Pensnett, nr Dudley, 3 November 1920. Educated at Gilbert Claughton Grammar School, Dudley.
Debut 1952 v Cambridge U, Worcester 1952. 1 match for W (amateur) 1952. 4* in only innings.
Birmingham League cricket for Dudley.

GORDON, Herbert Prichard – RHB RM
b. Bridgnorth, Shrops. 13 September 1898; d. Brighton, 17 October 1965. Educated at Malvern.
Debut 1923 v W. Indies, Worcester. 7 matches for W (amateur) 1923–24. Highest score: W 68* v W. Indies, Worcester 1923 (on debut).

GRAVENEY, Thomas William – RHB LB
b. Riding Mill, Northumb., 16 June 1927. Educated at Bristol Grammar School.

T.W. Graveney

Debut 1961 v Australia, Worcester 1961. 208 matches for W 1961–70. Cap 1962, captain 1968–70; benefit (£7,886) 1969. Highest score: W 166 v Essex, Worcester 1966. Best bowling: W 2–10 v Oxford U, Oxford 1970. 1000 runs (7) – 2375 (55.23) 1964 best. Shares W 3rd wicket partnership record with M.J. Horton; 314 v Som., Worcester 1962.

Played 296 matches Glos., 1948–60; cap 1948; captain 1959–60; benefit (£5,400) 1959. 7 matches for Queensland 1969/70–1971/72. Best first-class bowling 5–28 Glos. v Derby., Bristol 1953. 79 tests for England, 1951–69. Highest score tests (and first-class) 258 v W. Indies, Trent Bridge 1957. 4882 test runs (44.38); 11 centuries. 47793 first-class runs (44.91); 122 centuries; 550 catches; 80 wickets (37.96). Seven first-class double centuries in career. Four times two centuries in a match. Only batsman to score more than 10000 runs for two counties (W and Glos). First batsman to score 30000 runs and 100 centuries in purely post-war cricket. Birmingham League cricket for Dudley.

Author *Cricket through the Covers* (1958); *Cricket over Forty* (1970). Now a regular summariser on BBC cricket transmissions. Awarded OBE for services to cricket. Brother Ken, and nephew David both Glos.

J.W. Greenstock

GREENSTOCK, John Wilfrid – RHB SLA
b. Great Malvern, 15 May 1905. Educated at Malvern and Brasenose College, Oxford U.

Debut 1924 v Northants, Worcester. 13 matches W 1924–27 (amateur). Highest score: W 23* v Hants, Bournemouth 1925. Best bowling: W 4–69 v Som., Taunton 1924.

31 matches Oxford U 1925–27 (Blue each season). Highest first-class score: 43 Oxford U v Essex, Chelmsford 1927. Best first-class bowling: 5–36 Oxford U v the Army, Oxford 1926. 507 first-class runs (9.38); 139 wickets (26.34).

Father Wm. Greenstock (W and Cambridge U).

GREENSTOCK, William – RHB OB
b. Keiskama Hoek, Cape Province, S. Africa, 15 January 1865; d. Dogmersfield, Hants, 13 November 1944. Educated at Fettes and Cambridge U.

Debut 1899 v Derby., Derby 1899. 4 matches for W 1899–1919 (amateur). Highest score: W 33 v H.K. Foster's XI, Worcester 1919.

3 matches for Cambridge U 1886–87.

Son J.W. Greenstock (Oxford U and W).

G.C. Griffiths

K. Griffith

GREENWOOD, Leonard Warwick – RHB
b. Liverpool, 25 March 1899; d. Astley, Stourport, 20 July 1982.
Educated at Winchester and Oxford U.
   Debut 1922 v Lancs., Worcester. 3 matches for W (amateur) 1922–26.
Highest score: W 25 v Glos., Worcester 1925.

GREIG, Geoffrey George Fenner – RHB RF
b. Blything, Suffolk, 15 August 1897. d. Ewhurst, Surrey, 24 October
1960. Educated at Westminster and Oxford U.
   Debut 1920 v Hants, Worcester. 18 matches W (amateur) 1920–25.
Highest score: W 37 v Hants, Worcester 1920. Best bowling: W 7–86 v
Lancs., Old Trafford 1920.

GRIFFITH, Kevin – RHB OB
b. Warrington, Ches., 17 January 1950. Educated at Worcester Royal
Grammar School.
   Debut 1967 v Lancs., Worcester 1967. 44 matches for W 1967–72.
Highest score: W 59 v Yorks., Sheffield 1971. Best bowling: W 7–41 v
Oxford U, Oxford 1969.
   Birmingham League for Kidderminster.

GRIFFITHS, Gordon Craven – RHB WK
b. Birmingham, 19 June 1905. Educated at Malvern.
   Debut 1932 v Lancs., Worcester. 5 matches for W (amateur) 1932–35.
Highest score: W 16 v Lancs., Worcester 1932 (debut).

V. Grimshaw

C.W.C. Grove

GRIMSHAW, Vernon – RHB LB
b. Leeds, 15 April 1916. d. Beds., 21 June 1989.

Debut 1936 v Lancs., Old Trafford. 19 matches for W 1936–38 (professional). Highest score: W 103 v New Zealand, Worcester 1937.

Minor Counties for Beds., 1955.

GRISEWOOD, Frederick Henry ('Freddie') – RHB
b. Daylesford, 11 April 1888; d. Hindhead, Surrey, 15 November 1972. Educated at Radley and Magdalen College, Oxford U.

Debut 1908 v Oxford U, Oxford. 1 match for W (amateur) 1908. Scored 6* and 1 in only match.

A well-known broadcaster; best known as chairman of *Any Questions*.

GROVE, Charles William Collard – RHB RMF
b. Birmingham, 16 December 1912; d. Solihull, War., 15 February 1982. Educated at Yardley Secondary School.

Debut 1954 v Pakistan, Worcester. 15 matches for W 1954 (professional). Highest score: W 25 v Pakistan, Worcester 1954 (debut). Best bowling: W 8–66 v Glos., Worcester 1954.

201 matches for War., 1938–53. Cap 1947; benefit (£4,464) 1951.

Highest first-class score: 104* War. v Leics., Leicester 1948. Best
first-class bowling: 9–39 War. v Sussex, Edgbaston 1952. 3161 first-class
runs (11.57); 744 first-class wickets (22.66). Birmingham League cricket
for Mitchells & Butlers, Old Hill, Smethwick.

At time of death was War. scorer.

HALL, Brian Charles – RHB RM
b. Edgware, London, 2 March 1934. Educated at Gregg's Commercial Coll., Marylebone.

Debut 1956 v Oxford U, Worcester 1956. 3 matches for W 1956–57 (professional). Highest score: W 21 v Oxford U, Worcester 1956 (debut). Best bowling: W 2–11 same match.

Club cricket for Stanmore.

HAMPTON, William Marcus – RHB SRA
b. Bromsgrove, 20 January 1903. d. Ringwood, Hants, 7 April 1964. Educated at Clifton College and Emmanuel College, Cambridge U.

Debut 1925 v Glam., Worcester. 12 matches for W 1925–26 (amateur). Highest score: W 57 v War., Dudley 1925.

1 match for War. 1922.

Assistant master at Winchester for many years.

W.M. Hampton

B.C. Hall

D.P. Harkness

H. Harper

HARBER, John – RHB
b. Malvern Wells, 12 November 1889; d. Croome, 11 August 1962.
   Debut 1914 v Derby., Worcester. 1 match for W (amateur) 1914.
Scored 3 and 0 in only match. Best bowling: W 2–24 in only match.

HARKNESS, Donald Peter – LHB ROB
b. Sydney, Australia, 13 February 1931.
   Debut 1954 v Oxford U, Oxford. 13 matches for W (professional)
1954. Highest score: W 163 v Cambridge U, Worcester 1954. Best
bowling: W 3–29 v Notts., Trent Bridge 1954.
   Birmingham League cricket for Kidderminster.

HARPER, Herbert ('Harry') – RHB
b. Birmingham, 1 February 1889; d. Birmingham, 6 August 1983.
   Debut 1920 v Yorks., Worcester. 1 match for W (amateur) 1920.
Scored 7 and 3 in only match.
   Birmingham League cricket for Handsworth Wood, later played
Moseley Ashfield.
   In later years a member of Warwickshire Youth Cricket Council.

HARRIS, George Cecil – LF Tail end batsman
b. Droitwich, 3 March 1906.
   Debut 1925 v Notts., Trent Bridge. 4 matches for W 1925
(professional). Highest score: W 4 v Derby., Chesterfield 1925. Best
bowling: W 2–40 v Derby., Chesterfield 1925.

F. Harry

C.S. Harrison

HARRISON, Cyril Stanley – LHB SLA
b. Droitwich, 11 November 1915. Educated at Worcester Royal Grammar School.

Debut W 1934 v Lancs., Worcester. 17 matches for W 1934–35 (amateur). Highest score: W 28 v Lancs., Blackpool 1934. Best bowling: W 7–51 v Hants, Worcester 1934.

HARRY, Frank – RHB RMF
b. Newton Abbot, 22 December 1876; d. Great Malvern, 27 October 1925.

Debut 1919 v Glos., Worcester. 7 matches for W 1919–20 (amateur). Highest score: W 14* v Glos., Cheltenham 1919. Best bowling: W 3–60 v Som., Worcester 1919.

69 matches Lancs as professional 1903–08. Highest first-class score: 88, Lancs v W, Worcester 1906. Best first-class bowling: 9–44 (15–70 match) Lancs. v War., Old Trafford 1906. Professional with Kilmarnock CC after leaving Lancs. in 1908. Later played for South Shields and appeared for Durham in Minor Counties Championship 1912–14.

Rugby League football for Broughton Rangers.

HARTILL, William Norman – RHB
b. Dudley, 12 December 1911; d. Martley, 3 March 1971.

Debut 1935 v Som., Dudley. 1 match for W (amateur) 1935. 2 runs in only innings.

Birmingham League cricket for Dudley.

HEADLEY, Ronald George Alphonso – LHB LB

b. Kingston, Jamaica, 29 June 1939,

Debut 1958 v Cambridge U, Worcester. 403 matches for W 1958–74. Cap 1961; benefit (£10,014) 1972. Highest score: W 187 v Northants, Worcester 1971. Best bowling: W 4–40 v Glam., Worcester 1963. 1000 runs (12) 2026 (32.67) 1961 best. Scored 187 and 108, W v Northants, Worcester 1971.

Played for Jamaica 1965/66–1973/74. 2 tests for W. Indies v England 1973. Highest test score: 42, the Oval 1973. Birmingham League cricket for Dudley, Old Hill.

Father George Headley (W. Indies); son, Dean Headley on W staff.

HEMSLEY, Edward John Orton – RHB RM

b. Norton, Stoke-on-Trent, 1 September 1943. Educated at Bridgnorth Grammar School.

Debut 1963 v Pakistani Eaglets, Worcester. 243 matches for W 1963–82. Cap 1969; benefit 1982. Highest score: W 176* v Lancs., Worcester 1977. Best bowling: W 3–5 v War., Worcester 1971. 1000 runs

R.G.A. Headley

E.J.O. Hemsley

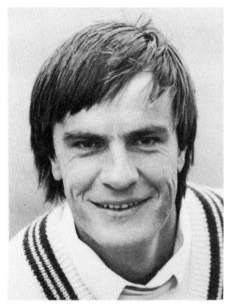

S.P. Henderson

G.A. Hick

(1) – 1168 (38.93) in 1978. Added 227 for 6th wicket with D.N. Patel v Oxford U, Oxford 1976 – 6th wicket record until 1988.

Played Shrops. in Minor Counties Championship 1961. Birmingham League cricket for Stourbridge.

Professional soccer for Shrewsbury, Sheffield United, Doncaster Rovers.

HENDERSON, Stephen Peter – LHB RM
b. Oxford, 24 September 1958. Educated at Downside and Durham U and Magdalene College, Cambridge U.

Debut 1977 v Glam., Worcester (obtained a 'pair'). 24 matches for W 1977–81. Highest score: W 64 v Lancs., Stourport 1980.

19 matches for Cambridge U 1982–83 (Blue both seasons). 27 matches for Glam. 1983–85. Highest first-class score: 209* Cambridge U v Middx., Cambridge 1982 (his maiden century). Minor Counties Championship for Shropshire (1982), Hertfordshire since 1987. Birmingham League cricket for Dudley and Worcester City.

Father D. Henderson (Oxford Blue).

HICK, Graeme Ashley – RHB OB
b. Salisbury, Rhodesia (now Harare, Zimbabwe), 23 May 1966. Educated at Prince Edward High School, Salisbury.

Debut 1984 v Surrey, The Oval (scoring 82*). 95 matches for W 1984–date. Highest score: W 405* v Som., Taunton 1988 (W record). Best bowling: W 5–52 v Essex, Colchester 1989. Shared W partnership record for 2nd wicket – 287* with T.S. Curtis v Glam., Neath 1986, 6th wicket – 265 with S.J. Rhodes v Som., Taunton 1988, 7th wicket – 205 with P.J. Newport v Yorks., Worcester 1988 and 8th wicket – 177* with R.K. Illingworth v Som., Taunton 1988. 1000 runs (4) – 2615 (79.24) 1988 best. 10 centuries in season 1988 – shares record with G.M. Turner.

Played Zimbabwe 1983–85. Northern Districts (NZ) 1987/88–88/89. At end of 1989 season had scored 12733 runs in first-class cricket, average 60.92.

HICKTON, William Henry – RHB SLA
b. Lower Broughton, Lancs., 28 August 1885; d. Leeds, 8 April 1942.

Debut 1909 v Yorks., Worcester. 5 matches for W (professional) 1909. Highest score: W 17 v Middx., Worcester 1909. Best bowling: W 1–9 v Middx., Worcester 1909.

Birmingham League cricket for Stourbridge.

HIGGINS, Harry Leslie – RHB
b. Bournville, 24 February 1894; d. Malvern, 19 September 1979. Educated at King Edwards, Birmingham.

Debut 1920 v Som., Taunton. 97 matches for W (amateur) 1920–27. Highest score: W 137* v Lancs., Worcester 1922. 1000 runs (2) – 1182 (28.82) 1921 best.

Birmingham League cricket for Kidderminster. Brother J.B. Higgins (W).

H.L. Higgins

J.B. Higgins

J.G. Higginson

HIGGINS, John Bernard – RHB SLA

b. Harborne, Birmingham, 31 December 1885; d. Malvern, 3 January 1970. Educated at King Edwards, Birmingham.

Debut 1912 v Leics., Stourbridge. 111 matches for W (amateur) 1912–30. Highest score: W 123 v Glam., Kidderminster 1927. Best bowling: W 5–72 v Glos., Gloucester 1922. 1041 runs (30.61) in 1928.

Minor Counties for Staffs. 1909.

Brother H.L. Higgins (W).

HIGGINSON, J.G. – RHB RF

b. W January 1885; d. Wolverhampton, September 1940.

Debut 1912 v Som., Stourbridge. 1 match for W (amateur) 1912. 0* in only innings.

Was a schoolmaster from Brierley Hill and played Birmingham League cricket for Stourbridge.

HIGGS-WALKER, James Arthur – RHB RFM

b. Clent, 31 July 1892. d. Midhurst, Sussex, 3 September 1979. Educated at Repton and St John's College, Oxford U.

Debut 1913 v Glos., Cheltenham. 2 matches for W (amateur) 1913–19. Highest score: W 44 v War., Edgbaston 1919. Best bowling: W 1–69 v War., Edgbaston 1919.

Master at Sevenoaks school.

D.V. Hill

J.A. Higgs-Walker

HILL, Denys Vivian – RHB RF
b. Edmonton, Middx., 13 April 1896; d. Barton-on-Sea, Hants, 15 May
1971.
　Debut 1927 v Kent, Folkestone. 28 matches for W 1927–29 (amateur).
Highest score: W 38 v Glam., Worcester 1928. Best bowling: W 6–59 v
Northants, Northampton 1927.
　Played first-class cricket for the Army 1922–26.

HILL, W.H. – B
Debut 1900 v Lancs., Old Trafford. 2 matches for W (amateur) 1900.
Highest score: W 13* v Hants, Worcester 1900.

Ron Headley and Glenn Turner take the field at the start of the innings.

V.A. Holder

H.O. Hopkins

HOLDER, Vanburn Alonzo – RHB RFM
b. St Michael, Barbados, 8 October 1945.
    Debut 1968 v Oxford U, Oxford. 181 matches for W 1968–80. Cap 1970; benefit 1979. Highest score: W 52 v Glos., Dudley 1970. Best bowling: W 7–40 v Glam., Cardiff 1974.
    Played Barbados 1966/67–77/78. Played Orange Free State 1985/86. Highest score, all first-class cricket: 122, Barbados v Trinidad, Bridgetown 1973/74. 40 tests for W. Indies 1969–1978/79; Highest test score: 42 v New Zealand, Port-of-Spain 1971/72. Best test bowling: 6–28 v Australia, Port-of-Spain 1977/78. Test record: 682 runs (14.20): 109 wickets (33.27). Minor Counties Championship for Shrops. 1981. Birmingham League cricket for West Bromwich Dartmouth.

HOLYOAKE, Ronald Hubert –
b. Droitwich, 1894; d. Droitwich, 8 November 1966.
    Debut W 1924 v Som., Taunton. 3 matches for W (amateur) 1924. Highest score: W 22 v Notts., Worcester 1922.

HOPKINS, Herbert Oxley – RHB
b. Adelaide, S. Australia, 6 July 1895; d. Milverton, Som., 23 February 1972. Educated at St Peter's College, Adelaide and Oxford U.
    Debut 1921 v Glam., Swansea. 63 matches for W 1921–31 (amateur). Highest score: W 137 v Notts., Trent Bridge 1924. Best bowling: W 2–23 v Notts., Trent Bridge 1924.
    21 matches for Oxford U 1921–23; Blue 1923. Highest first-class score: 142* Oxford U v the Army, Oxford 1922. 3204 first-class runs (22.41).

A medical practitioner who spent much of his time in the Malay States and was virtually lost to first-class cricket after leaving university.

HORTON, Henry – RHB
b. Colwall Green, Herefordshire, 18 April 1923.

Debut 1946 v RAF, Worcester. 11 matches for W 1946–49 (professional). Highest score: W 21 v Combined Services, Hereford 1947.

405 matches for Hants 1953–67. Cap 1955; benefit 1964. Highest first-class score: 160* Hants v Yorks., Scarborough 1961. Scored 1000 runs in season 12 times; 2428 (47.60) in 1959 best.

First-class umpire 1973–75. Played professional soccer for Blackburn Rovers, Southampton, Bradford. Brother Joseph Horton (W).

HORTON, Joseph – RHB RM
b. Colwall Green, Herefordshire, 12 August 1916.

Debut 1934 v Derby., Chesterfield 1934. 62 matches for W (professional) 1934–38. Highest score: W 70 v Glam., Worcester 1938. Best bowling: W 2–3 v Derby., Worcester 1935.

Played for Hereford. Brother Henry Horton (W).

J. Horton

H. Horton

M.J. Horton

HORTON, Martin John – RHB OB
b. Worcester, 21 April 1934.
   Debut 1952 v Oxford U, Oxford. 376 matches for W (professional) 1952–66. Cap 1955; benefit (£5,860) 1965. Highest score: W 233 v Som., Worcester 1962. Best bowling: W 9–56 v S. Africa, Worcester 1955. During highest score above added 314 for 3rd wicket with T.W. Graveney – county record. Carried bat for 53*/91 v Lancs., Old Trafford 1966. 1000 runs (11) – 2123 (44.22) 1959 best. Hat trick v Som., Bath 1956. Achieved 'double' in 1961; 1808 runs (29.16); 101 wickets (21.12).
   Played Northern Districts (NZ) 1967/68–1970/71; New Zealand National Coach 1966–84. 2 tests for England v India 1959. Highest test score 58. Best test bowling 2–24. 19945 first-class runs (29.54); 23 100s; 825 wickets (26.94). Birmingham League cricket for Stourbridge.
   Lately coach, Worcester Royal Grammar School.

HOWARD, Joseph – RHB
b. Epsom, Surrey, 12 January 1881; d. Evenlode, Glos., 25 January 1951. Educated at Haileybury.
   Debut 1900 v Yorks., Bradford. 5 matches for W 1900–01 (amateur). Highest score: W 28 v MCC, Lord's 1901.

Martin Horton

R. Howorth

N. Hughes

HOWORTH, Richard – LHB SLA
b. Bacup, Lancs., 26 April 1909; d. Worcester, 2 April 1980.

Debut 1933 v W. Indies, Worcester. 348 matches for W (professional) 1933–51. Cap 1934: benefit (£3,000) 1949. Highest score: W 114 v Kent, Dover 1936. Best bowling: W 7–18 (10–57 match) v Northants, Kettering 1949. Added 197 for 7th wicket with H.H.I.H. Gibbons v Surrey, the Oval 1938; W record until 1988. 1000 runs (3) – 1172 (24.93) 1947 best. 100 wickets (9) – 138 (16.09) 1947 best. 'Double' twice – 1019 runs (21.23) and 111 wkts (24.34) 1939. 1172 runs (24.93) and 138 wkts (16.09) 1947. W committee after retirement.

5 tests for England 1947–47/48; highest test score; 45* v S. Africa, the Oval 1947; best test bowling 6–124 v W. Indies, Bridgetown 1947/48. 145 test runs (18.12); 19 test wickets (33.42). 11479 first-class runs (20.68); 1345 wickets (21.87). Birmingham League cricket for Stourbridge, Walsall, Old Hill.

HUGHES, Noel – RHB OB occasional WK
b. Sydney, Australia, 6 April 1929.

Debut 1953 v Cambridge U, Cambridge. 21 matches W 1953–54 (professional). Highest score: W 95 v Essex, Worcester 1954. Best bowling: W 4–19 v Hants, Portsmouth 1954.

HUGHES, Richard Clive – LHB LFM
b. Watford, Herts., 30 September 1926. Educated at Watford Grammar School.
Debut 1950 v Combined Services, Worcester. 11 matches W 1950–51 (professional). Highest score: W 21 v Surrey, The Oval 1951. Best bowling: W 3–38 v Combined Services, Worcester 1950.
Played Herts. 1953–59.

HUMAN, Roger Henry Charles – RHB RM
b. Newcastle-on-Tyne, 11 May 1909. d. in action, Bangalore, India, 21 November 1942. Educated at Repton and Emmanuel College, Cambridge U.
Debut 1934 v Cambridge U, Cambridge. 39 matches for W 1934–39 (amateur). Highest score: W 81 v Essex, Worcester 1938. Best bowling: W 2–51 v Essex, Worcester 1938.
18 matches for Cambridge U 1930–31 (Blue both seasons). Best first-class bowling: 4–42 Cambridge U v MCC, Lord's 1930. 2236 first-class runs (24.57); 51 wickets (38.17). Minor Counties Championship, Berks. 1928–34.
Qualified for W while teaching at Bromsgrove School. Brother J.H. Human (Middx. and Cambridge U).

HUMPHERSON, Victor William – RHB RM
b. Bewdley, 15 July 1896; d. Rowfant, Sussex, 19 October 1978.
Debut 1921 v War., Worcester 1921. 13 matches for W (amateur) 1921–23. Highest score: W 16 v War., Worcester 1921 on debut. Best bowling: W 5–50 v Glos., Clifton 1921.

R.H.C. Human

C.A. Humphries

D.J. Humphries

HUMPHRIES, Cedric Alfred – RHB RM
b. Kidderminster, 26 December 1914; d. in action, in Holland, 18 November 1944. Educated at Sebright School and Downing College, Cambridge U. Debut 1934 v Lancs., Worcester. 13 matches for W 1934–35 (amateur). Highest score: W 44 v Cambridge U, Worcester 1934. Birmingham League for Kidderminster.
　　Brothers G.H. and N.H. Humphries (W).

HUMPHRIES, David John – LHB WK
b. Aveley, Shrops., 6 August 1953. Educated at Bridgnorth Sec. School; Wulfrun College, Wolverhampton.
　　Debut 1977 v Sussex, Worcester. 170 matches W 1977–85. Highest score: W 133 v Derby., Worcester 1984. 8 dismissals in match (7 ct 1 st) v Derby., Derby 1979 (equalled county record at the time for County Championship).
　　5 matches for Leics 1974–76. Minor Counties Championship for Shrops. 1971–73. Birmingham League cricket for West Bromwich Dartmouth and Worcester City.

HUMPHRIES, Gerald Harvey – RHB RM
b. Kidderminster, 8 December 1908; d. Rock, near Kidderminster, 3 February 1983.
　　Debut 1932 v Sussex, Kidderminster. 2 matches for W 1932–34 (amateur). Highest score W 36 v Glam., Cardiff 1934.

F. Hunt   *M. Hussain*

Birmingham League cricket for Kidderminster. President of Birmingham League 1976. Brothers C.A. and N.H. Humphries.

HUMPHRIES, Norman Hampton – RHB LB
b. Kidderminster, 19 May 1917.
Debut 1946 v War., Edgbaston. 7 matches for W 1946 (amateur). Highest score (W) 22 v Glam., Dudley 1946.
Minor Counties for Devon, 1947–55. Birmingham League cricket for Kidderminster. Brothers C.A. and G.H. Humphries (W).

HUNT, Frederick – RHB RM
b. Aldworth, Berks., 13 September 1875; d. Worcester, 31 March 1967.
Debut 1900 v London County, Worcester. 53 matches for W (professional) 1900–22. Highest score: W 40* v Philadelphians, Worcester 1908. Best bowling: W 4–36 v Essex, Leyton 1910.
6 matches for Kent 1897–98.
Worcester groundsman 1898–1946.

HUSSAIN, Mehriyar – RHB OB
b. South Shields, 17 October 1963.
Debut 1985 v Cambridge U, Cambridge. 1 match for W 1985. Scored 4 in only innings.
Brother N. Hussain (Essex).

W.E.C. Hutchings

HUTCHINGS, William Edward Colebrook – RHB
b. Southborough, Kent, 31 May 1879; d. Prees, near Whitchurch, Shrops., 8 March 1948. Educated at Tonbridge.

Debut 1905 v Lancs., Liverpool. 22 matches for W (amateur) 1905–06. Highest score: W 85 v Kent, Tunbridge Wells 1905.

Played 2 matches, Kent 1899. Played Berks. (Minor Counties) 1901. Birmingham League cricket for Dudley.

Brothers K.L. Hutchings (Kent and England) and F.V. Hutchings (Kent).

ILLINGWORTH, Richard Keith – RHB SLA
b. Greengates, Bradford, 23 August 1963. Educated at Wroze Brow Middle; Salts Grammar School.

Debut 1982 v Som., Worcester. 187 matches for W 1982–date. Cap 1986. Highest score: W 120* v War., Worcester 1987. Best bowling: W 7–50 v Oxford U, Oxford 1985. Shares W's record stand for 7th wicket with G.A. Hicks – 177* v Som., Taunton 1988.

Birmingham League cricket for Worcester City.

IMRAN KHAN NIAZI – RHB RF
b. Lahore, Pakistan, 25 November 1952. Educated at Aitchison College,

R.K. Illingworth

K.N. Imran

J.D. Inchmore

Lahore; Cathedral School, Lahore; Worcester Royal Grammar School; Keble College, Oxford U.

Debut 1971 v India, Worcester 1971. 42 matches for W 1971–76. Highest score: W 166 v Northants, Northampton 1976. Best bowling: W 7–53 v Lancs., Worcester 1976.

Played for Sussex 1977–88; cap 1978; benefit 1987. 24 matches Oxford U 1973–75; Blue each season. Captain 1975. 75 tests for Pakistan 1971–87/88 (captain 35 times). Highest test score: 135* v India, Madras 1986/87. Best test bowling: 8–58 (14–116 match) v Sri Lanka, Faisalabad 1981/82. Became third player after I.T. Botham and Kapil Dev to complete test 'double' of 3000 runs and 300 wickets in 1987/88. Test career record: 3000 runs (33.70); 4 centuries; 341 wickets (22.04). Has played domestic cricket in Pakistan for various Lahore teams since 1969/70. Match doubles: 111* 7–53, 6–46, W v Lancs., Worcester 1976; 117 6–98, 5–82 Pakistan v India, Faisalabad 1982/83. Hat trick – Sussex v War., Edgbaston 1983. Highest first-class score: 170, Oxford U v Northants, Oxford 1974. Best first-class bowling: 8–34 Sussex v Middx., Lord's 1986.

INCHMORE, John Darling – RHB RFM
b. Ashington, Northumb., 22 February 1949. Educated at Ashington Grammar School.

Debut 1973 v New Zealand, Worcester. 216 matches for W 1973–86. Cap 1976; benefit 1985. Highest score: W 113 v Essex, Worcester 1974. Best bowling: W 8–58 v Yorks., Worcester 1977.

Birmingham League cricket for Stourbridge.

ISAAC, Arthur Whitmore – RHB
b. Powick, 4 October 1873; d. in action, Contalmaison, France, 7 July 1916. Educated at Harrow and Oxford U.
Debut 1899 v Oxford U, Oxford. 52 matches for W 1899–1911 (amateur). Highest score: W 60 v Hants, Southampton 1904. Served on Worcs CCC committee and as Hon. Treasurer.
Club cricket for Worcester St John's.
Brother J.E.V. Isaac (W). Son H.W. Isaac (W).

ISAAC, Herbert Whitmore – RHB
b. Worcester, 11 December 1899; d. Chisekesi, N. Rhodesia, 26 April 1962. Educated at Harrow.
Debut 1919 v War., Edgbaston. 3 matches for W 1919 (amateur). Highest score: W 23 v H.K. Foster's XI, Worcester 1919.
Father A.W. Isaac (W); uncle J.E.V. Isaac (W).

ISAAC, John Edward Valentine – RHB
b. Upton-on-Severn, 14 February 1880; d. in action, Armentières, France, 9 May 1915. Educated at Harrow.

A.W. Isaac

H.W. Isaac

D. Isles

Debut 1907 v Oxford U, Oxford. 4 matches for W (amateur) 1907. Highest score: W 13 v Oxford U, Oxford 1907.

Played first-class cricket for the Army v MCC at Roberts' Heights, S. Africa 1904/05; also 4 matches for Orange River Colony in 1906/07 Currie Cup. Highest first-class score 34*, ORC v Western Province, Pretoria 1906/07.

A good horseman, won the Cairo Grand National in 1911. Brother A.W. Isaac (W).

ISLES, Derek – RHB WK

b. Bradford, 14 October 1943.

Debut 1967 v Pakistan, Worcester. 1 match for W 1967. Highest score: W 17* v Pakistan 1967.

Played for Undercliffe and Bingley clubs.

J

JACKSON, John Frederick Cecil – RHB
b. Aylesford, Kent, 1880; d. Blakedown, W, 1968. Educated at Tonbridge.
Debut 1907 v Oxford U, Oxford. 1 match for W (amateur) 1907. Highest score W 6 in only match.

JACKSON, Percy Frederick ('Peter') – RHB OB
b. Aberfeldy, Perthshire, Scotland, 11 May 1911.
Debut 1929 v Lancs., Worcester. 383 matches for W 1929–50 (professional). Cap 1931; benefit (£2,150) 1948. Highest score: W 40 v Glos., Worcester 1933. Best bowling: W 9–45 v Som., Dudley 1935. 100 wickets (4) 118 (19.61) 1946 best.
Birmingham League for Old Hill.

P.F. Jackson

R.O. Jenkins

E.P. Jeavons

JAGGER, Samuel Thornton – RHB RM
b. Llangollen, Denbighs., Wales, 30 June 1904; d. Hove, Sussex, 30 May 1964. Educated at Malvern and Clare College, Cambridge U.

Debut 1922 v Som., Weston-super-Mare. 5 matches for W 1922–23 (amateur). Highest score: W 41 v Hants, Worcester 1923. Best bowling: W 3–25 v Essex, Leyton 1924.

29 matches Cambridge U 1923–26 (Blue 1925, 1926). Played 3 matches for Sussex 1931. 3 matches for Wales 1927–29. Highest first-class score: 58 Cambridge U v Essex, Colchester 1923. Best first-class bowling: 5–24 Cambridge U v Yorks., Cambridge 1926. First-class record: 599 runs (11.30); 90 wickets (33.77).

JEAVONS, Enoch Percy – RHB
b. Dudley, 1893; d. Dudley, 1967.

Debut 1924 v Glos., Dudley. 1 match for W 1924 (amateur). Highest score: W 1* only match.

Birmingham League cricket for Dudley.

JENKINS, Roland Oliver ('Roly') – RHB LBG
b. Worcester, 24 November 1918.

Debut 1938 v Essex, Southend. 352 matches for W 1938–58 (professional). Cap 1939: benefit (£3,411) 1953. Highest score: W 109 v

Notts., Trent Bridge 1948. Best bowling: W 8–62 (15–122 match) v Sussex, Dudley 1953. 1000 runs (2) – 1310 (28.4) 1948 best. 100 wickets (5) – 159 (20.84) 1949 best. Three hat tricks – all against Surrey; the Oval 1948, and each innings at Worcester 1949.

9 tests for England 1948/49–52. Highest test score: 39 v W. Indies, Trent Bridge 1950. Best test bowling: 5–116 v W. Indies, Lord's 1950. Test record: 198 runs (18.00): 32 wickets (34.31). First-class record: 10073 runs (22.23); 1309 wickets (23.64). Birmingham League cricket for West Bromwich Dartmouth.

Nephew P.J. Robinson (W and Somerset).

JEWELL, Arthur North – RHB WK

b. Iquique, Chile, 1888; d. Selsey, Sussex, 8 September 1922. Educated at Felsted. Debut 1919 v H.K. Foster's XI, Hereford 1919. 22 matches for W 1919–20 (amateur). Highest score: W 128 v H.K. Foster's XI, Worcester 1919. Five matches for Orange Free State, 1910/11 Currie Cup. 946 first-class runs (16.89).

Brothers M.F.S. Jewell (W) and J.E. Jewell (Orange Free State). Nephew J.M.H. Jewell (W).

JEWELL, John Mark Herbert – RHB

b. Bloemfontein, S. Africa, 1917; d. Durban, S. Africa, 29 October 1946. Educated at Felsted.

Debut 1939 v W. Indies, Worcester 1939. 2 matches for W (amateur) 1939. Highest score: W 24 v W. Indies, Worcester 1939 on debut.

Father J.E. Jewell (Orange Free State); uncles M.F.S. Jewell and A.N. Jewell (W).

M.F.S. Jewell

A.N. Jewell

E.P. Jobson

JEWELL, Maurice Francis Stewart – RHB SLA
b. Iquique, Chile, 15 September 1885; d. Birdham, Sussex, 28 May 1978.
Educated at Marlborough.
   Debut 1909 v Oxford U, Oxford. 121 matches for W (amateur)
1909–33. Captain 1920–21, 1926, 1928–29. Highest score: W 125 v Hants,
Worcester, 1926. Best bowling: W 7–56 v War., Worcester 1919.
W President 1950–56.
   6 matches Sussex 1914–19 (in 1919 played for both W and Sussex in
first-class inter-county matches, thus breaking rule no. 1 of the County
Cricket Rules then in operation. First-class career record: 4114 runs
(18.36); 104 wickets (33.15).
   Brothers A.N. and J.E. Jewell (W and Orange Free State
respectively). Nephew J.M.H. Jewell (W); son M. Jewell (W II).

JOBSON, Edward Percy – RHB RM
b. Wall Heath, Staffs., 20 March 1855; d. Himley, Staffs., 20 April 1909.
   Debut 1900 v Sussex, Hove. 7 matches for W (amateur) 1900–03.
Highest score: W 26 v Oxford U, Oxford 1900.
   Played 1 game MCC 1891. Played for W County teams before
first-class status. Birmingham League cricket for Dudley.

JOHNSON, Ivan Nicholas – LHB SLA
b. Nassau, Bahamas, 27 June 1953. Educated at Malvern.
Debut 1972 v Oxford U, Oxford. 33 matches for W 1972–75. Highest
score: W 69 v Notts., Worcester 1975. Best bowling: W 5–74 v Oxford U,
Oxford 1975.

JOLLY, Norman William – B WK
b. Adelaide, S. Australia, 5 August 1882; d. probably in Australia, May
1954. Educated in Australia and Balliol College, Oxford U.
Debut 1907 v Oxford U, Oxford. 1 match for W (amateur) 1907.
Highest score: W 8 in only match.

JONES, Barry John Richardson – LHB RM
b. Shrewsbury, Shropshire, 2 November 1955. Educated at Wrekin
College.
Debut 1976 v Oxford U, Oxford 1976. 46 matches for W 1976–80.
Highest score: W 65 v War., Edgbaston 1977.
Played Shrops. in Minor Counties Championship 1981–82. Club:
Wroxeter. Birmingham League cricket for Dudley.

B.J.R. Jones

I.N. Johnson

R. Jones

JONES, Ronald – RHB
b. Wolverhampton, Staffs., 9 September 1938.
    Debut 1955 v Cambridge U, Worcester. 1 match for W (amateur)
1955. Highest score: W 23 in only match.
    Birmingham League cricket for Stourbridge.

KAPIL DEV, Ramlal Nikhanj – RHB RFM
b. Chandigarh, India, 6 January 1959. Educated at Punjab U.
Debut 1984 v Hants, Worcester, scoring 95 in first innings. 24 matches
for W 1984–85. Highest score: W 100 v Middx., Lord's 1985. Best
bowling: W 5–30 v Som., Worcester 1984.
16 matches Northants, 1981–83. Has played Ranji Trophy cricket for
Haryana since 1975/76. 99 test matches for India since 1978/79 – captain
on 34 occasions. Test record: 4087 runs (31.19): 347 wickets (29.02).
Only the second player to score 4000 runs and take 300 wickets in tests
(after I.T. Botham). Best bowling in test and first-class cricket 9–83,
India v W. Indies, Ahmadabad 1983/84. Highest score in tests: 163 v Sri
Lanka, Kanpur 1986/87. Highest score in first-class cricket: 193, Haryana
v Punjab, Chandigarh 1979/80. Hat trick for N. Zone v W. Zone in
Duleep Trophy, Delhi 1978/79. An outstanding limited overs
international performer, scored 175* v Zimbabwe at Tunbridge Wells in
1983 ICC Trophy.

R.N. Kapil Dev

D. Kenyon

J.W. Keene

KEENE, John William – LHB LAS
b. Mitcham, Surrey, 25 April 1873; d. Crichton, Midlothian, Scotland, 3 January 1931.

Debut 1903 v Sussex, Hove. 24 matches for W 1903–05 (professional). Highest score: W 12 v Kent, Canterbury 1903. Best bowling: W 6–22 v Leics., Leicester 1903.

Played 2 matches for Surrey 1897; 1 game for Scotland in 1907.

KENYON, Donald – RHB
b. Wordsley, Staffs., 15 May 1924. Educated at Audnam Senior School.

Debut 1946 v Surrey, Worcester. 589 matches for W (County record) 1946–67. Professional: cap 1947; benefit (£3,840) 1957; captain 1959–67; testimonial (£6,351) 1964. Highest score: W 259 v Yorks., Kidderminster 1956. 34490 runs (34.18) for W – county record. 70 centuries county record until beaten by G.M. Turner. 1000 runs (19 – county record) 2430 (55.22) 1954 best, Also 2278 runs (49.52) 1953, 2174 runs (45.29) 1950, 2160 runs (39.27) 1957, 2133 runs (41.82) 1951, 2126 runs (40.88) 1952. County record of 7 double centuries for W. Carried bat through innings – 103*/215 v Hants, Bournemouth 1955. Current President of W CCC.

8 test matches for England 1951/52–55. Highest test score: 87 v S. Africa, Trent Bridge 1955. 192 runs in tests (12.80). 37002 runs (33.63) and 74 centuries in first-class cricket. Was a test selector from 1965–72 and appointed MBE for services to cricket. Played Birmingham League cricket for Stourbridge.

KIMBER, Simon Julian Spencer – RHB RFM
b. Ormskirk, Lancs., 6 October 1963. Educated at Thomas More School, Durban, S. Africa.
    Debut 1985 v Oxford U, Oxford. 2 matches for W in 1985. Highest score: W 14* on debut. Best bowling: W 3–40 v Cambridge U, Cambridge 1985.
    Has played for Sussex since 1987. Played Natal 'B' in 1986/87. Highest first-class score 54, Sussex v Notts., Eastbourne 1987. Best first-class bowling 4–76, Natal B v E Province B, Uitenhage 1986/87. Birmingham League Cricket for Dudley.

KIMPTON, Roger Charles McDonald – RHB WK
b. Toorak, Australia, 21 September 1916. Educated at Melbourne U., Brasenose College, Oxford U.
    Debut 1937 v Notts., Dudley. 14 matches for W (amateur) 1937–49. Highest score: W 106 v Derby., Chesterfield 1936. Best bowling: W 2–20 v Leics., Hinckley 1937.
    40 matches Oxford U 1935–38; Blue 1935, 1937, 1938. Highest first-class score: 160, Oxford U v Glos., Oxford 1935. 3562 runs (35.27) in first-class career.
    Brother S.M. Kimpton (Oxford U).

R.C.M. Kimpton

S.J.S. Kimber

C.L. King

B.P. King

KING, Benjamin Philip ('Phil') – RHB occ. WK
b. Leeds, 22 April 1915; d. Bradford, 31 March 1970.
   Debut 1935 v Northants, Worcester. 80 matches for W (professional) 1935–39. Cap 1938. Highest score: W 124 v Hants, Worcester 1938. 1177 runs (22.63) in 1938. Played 37 matches for Lancs., 1946–47 (cap 1946). Highest first-class score: 145, Lancs. v Oxford U, Oxford 1946. 4124 first-class runs (22.05). Played in Yorks. League.
   Cricket and Rugby League correspondent for *The People*.

KING, Collis Llewellyn – RHB RM
b. Fairview, Barbados, 11 June 1951. Educated at Metropolitan High School, Bridgetown, Barbados.
   Debut 1983 v Som., Worcester. 2 matches for W 1983. Highest score: W 123 on debut. Best bowling: W 1–26 same match.
   Played Barbados 1972/73–1981/82. 16 matches for Glam. 1977. 9 tests for W. Indies 1976–80. Highest test score: 100* v New Zealand, Christchurch 1979/80. Scored 418 test runs (32.15). Played World Series (Kerry Packer) cricket 1977/78–1978/79. Toured S. Africa with W. Indian XIs 1977/78–1978/79, leading to his banning from W. Indian cricket. Highest first-class score: 163, W. Indies v Northants, Northampton 1976. Best first-class bowling: 5–91, Barbados v Jamaica, Bridgetown 1975/76. Played for Natal 1984/85 to 1986/87. 6770 first-class runs (38.24); 128 wickets (34.21).

Don Kenyon with D.K. Gaekwad, Captain of the India Touring Side 1952.

J.W. King

B.E. Krikken

KING, John William – RHB
b. Leicester, 21 January 1908; d. Narborough, Leics., 25 March 1953.
    Debut 1927 v Sussex, Hove. 40 matches for W (professional) 1927–28. Highest score: W 91 v Essex, Leyton 1927.
    Eight matches for Leics 1929. 1169 first-class runs (15.80).
    Uncle J.H. King (Leics.).

KRIKKEN, Brian Egbert – RHB WK
b. Horwich, Lancs., 26 August 1946.
    Debut 1969 v Cambridge U, Halesowen. 1 match for W 1969. 4 in only innings.
    2 matches for Lancs. 1966–67. Played for Westhoughton and Horwich Clubs.

L

LAMPITT, Stuart Richard – RHB RM
b. Wolverhampton, 29 July 1966. Educated at Kingswinford School, Dudley Technical School.

Debut 1985 v Cambridge U, Cambridge. 24 matches for W 1985–date. Highest score: W 46 v War., Worcester 1989. Best bowling: W 5–32 v Kent, Worcester 1989.

Birmingham League cricket for Dudley and Stourbridge.

LANCHBURY, Robert John – RHB
b. Evesham, 11 February 1950. Educated at Cheltenham Grammar School.

Debut 1973 v New Zealand, Worcester. 8 matches for W 1973–74. Highest score: W 50* v Oxford U, Oxford 1974.

5 matches Glos. 1971. Played Wilts. in Minor Counties Championship since 1984. Birmingham League cricket for Old Hill and Dudley.

S.R. Lampitt

R.J. Lanchbury

A.F. Lane

W.T. Larkham

LANE, Albert Frederick ('Spinney') – RHB OB
b. Rowley Regis, Staffs., 29 August 1885; d. Upper Fulbrook, War., 29 January 1948. (Death from natural causes – erroneously attributed to car accident in some sources.)

Debut 1914 v Derby., Derby. 45 matches for W; 1914 as professional, 1927–32 as amateur. Highest score: W 76 v Yorks., Worcester 1927. Best bowling: W 3–41 v Essex, Leyton 1927.

12 matches War. 1919–25 as amateur. Best first-class bowling: 4–56, War. v Northants, Northampton 1919. Played Staffs. in Minor Counties Championship 1910. Birmingham League cricket for Stourbridge and Aston Unity.

Helped organize cricket in Midlands during World War II.

LANG. S.M. – LHB SLA
Debut 1923 v Hants, Worcester. 8 matches for W 1923–24 (professional). Highest score: W 9* v Notts., Trent Bridge 1924. Best bowling: W 2–21 v Northants, Northampton 1923.

LARKHAM, William Trevor – RHB LB
b. Kidderminster, 10 November 1929. Educated at King Charles I Grammar School, Kidderminster.

Debut 1952 v Yorks., Worcester. 1 match for W 1952 (amateur). Scored 0 and 13 in only match. 1–64 in only innings bowled in.

Birmingham League cricket for Kidderminster.

LEATHERDALE, David Anthony – RHB RM
b. Bradford, 26 November 1967. Educated at Pudsey Grangefield School.
Debut 1988 v Leics., Leicester. 17 matches for W 1988–date. Highest score: W 34* v Kent, Folkestone 1988.
Birmingham League cricket for Kidderminster.

LEESON, Patrick George – RHB OB
b. Darjeeling, India, 17 July 1915. Educated at Malvern.
Debut 1936 v Northants, Kettering. 1 match for W (amateur) 1936. Scored 0 and 7 in only match.

LEGARD, Antony Ronald – RHB RM
b. Sialkot, India, 17 January 1912. Educated at Winchester and Trinity College, Oxford U.
Debut 1935 v Northants, Northampton. 1 match for W 1935. 4 and 18 in only match; 0 wickets.
31 matches Oxford U 1932–35 (Blue 1932, 1935). Played Bombay Presidency cricket for the Europeans 1943/44. Other matches Free Foresters and MCC 1948–52. Highest first-class score: 38, Oxford U v S. America, Oxford 1932. Best first-class bowling: 7–36 Oxford U v Cambridge U, Lord's 1935. 93 first-class wickets (30.03).
Became secretary of Delamere Golf Club.

D.A. Leatherdale

H.W. Lobban

J. Lister

LISTER, Joseph – RHB
b. Thirsk, Yorks., 14 May 1930. Educated at Cheltenham.

Debut 1954 v Cambridge U, Worcester. 21 matches for W 1954–59 (amateur). Highest score: W 99 v Kent, Worcester 1955. Assistant-Secretary 1954–55; W Secretary 1956–71.

Played Yorks. (2) 1954 (appeared for W and Yorks in same season). First-class debut for Combined Services in 1951. Yorks. Secretary 1972–date.

Played hockey for Yorks. Uncle George Macaulay played Yorks and England.

LOBBAN, Hartley W. ('Ken') – RHB RFM
b. Jamaica, 9 May 1922. Educated (as mature student) at Sunderland Polytechnic.

Debut 1952 v Sussex, Worcester (as amateur – professional in 1953). 17 matches for W 1952–54. Highest score: W 18 v Sussex, Worthing 1953. Best bowling: W 6–51 v Glam., Cardiff 1952.

Birmingham League cricket for Kidderminster. Played for various north-eastern clubs after leaving W.

A professional boxer known as 'Ken Lobban' prior to playing cricket; also Rugby Union for Kidderminster. Lately living in United States and teaching.

LORD, Gordon John – LHB SLA
b. Edgbaston, Birmingham, 25 April 1961. Educated at Warwick School and Durham U.

Debut 1987 v Som., Taunton. 41 matches for W 1987–date. Highest score: W 101 v Glos., Bristol 1988.

18 matches War. 1983–86. Highest first-class score 199 (maiden century – run out) v Yorks., Edgbaston 1985. Birmingham League cricket for Old Hill.

LOWE, William Walter – RHB RF
b. Stamford, Lincs., 17 November 1873; d. Hartley-Wintney, Hants, 26 May 1945. Educated at Malvern and Pembroke College, Cambridge U.

Debut 1899 v Sussex, Worcester. 39 matches for W 1899–1911 (amateur). Highest score: W 154 v Leics., Leicester 1901. Best bowling: W 3–76 v London County, Crystal Palace 1900.

12 matches for Cambridge U 1895–96 (Blue 1895). Best first-class bowling: 5–48 Cambridge U v Oxford U, Lord's 1895.

LYTTELTON, (Rev. Hon) Charles Frederick – RHB RF
b. London, 26 January 1887; d. Paddington, London, 3 October 1931. Educated at Eton and Cambridge U.

Debut 1906 v Glos., Worcester. 9 matches for W (amateur) 1906–10. Highest score: W 18* v War., Worcester 1908. Best bowling: W 3–60 v Som., Worcester 1909.

G.J. Lord

W.W. Lowe

C.J. Lyttelton

C.F. Lyttelton

21 matches Cambridge U, 1907–09. Blue 1908–1909. Highest first-class score: 25* Cambridge U v Lancs., Cambridge 1907. Best first-class bowling: 5–33 v Lancs., Cambridge 1907.

A member of well-known Lyttelton cricketing family.

LYTTELTON, Charles John (later 10th Viscount Cobham) – RHB RM b. London, 8 August 1909; d. London, 20 March 1977. Educated at Eton.

Debut 1932 v Glos., Worcester. 93 matches for W 1932–39 (amateur). Capt W 1936–39. Highest score: W 162 v Leics., Loughborough 1938. Best bowling: W 4–83 v S. Africa, Worcester 1935.

President of MCC 1954, Treasurer MCC 1963. Governor-General of New Zealand 1957–62, captained his own team v MCC, Auckland 1960/61.

Member of well-known Lyttelton cricketing family.

C.J. Lyttelton (1932–39) was captain of Worcestershire 1936–39. Succeeded as 10th Viscount Cobham in 1949.

McEVOY, Michael Stephen Anthony – RHB RM
b. Jorhat, Assam, India, 25 January 1956. Educated at Colchester Royal Grammar School and Borough Road College of Education.

Debut 1983 v Yorks., Worcester. 26 matches for W 1983–84. Highest score: W 103 v War., Edgbaston 1983.

43 matches for Essex 1976–81. Best first-class bowling: 3–20, Essex v Middx., Lord's 1981. 2128 first-class runs (19.17). Played Minor Counties cricket Cambs., 1982; Suffolk since 1985. Birmingham League cricket for Kidderminster.

McEWAN, Stephen Michael – RHB RFM
b. Worcester, 5 May 1962. Educated at Worcester Royal Grammar School.

M.S.A. McEvoy

S.M. McEwan

Debut 1985 v Oxford U, Oxford. 40 matches for W 1985–date. Highest score: W 28* v War., Worcester. Best bowling: W 6–34 v Leics., Worcester 1989.

Birmingham League cricket for Worcester City, Kidderminster and Moseley.

MACLEAN, John Francis – RHB WK

b. Alnwick, Northumb., 1 March 1901; d. Ross-on-Wye, Herefordshire, 9 March 1986. Educated at Eton.

Debut 1922 v War., Edgbaston. 45 matches for W (amateur) 1922–24. Highest score: W 121 v Notts., Worksop 1923.

6 matches Glos., 1930–32.

MANN, William Horace – RHB

b. Melksham, Wilts., 28 July 1878; d. Canford Cliffs, Dorset, 24 February 1938. Educated at Marlborough.

Debut 1924 v Hants., Worcester. 1 match for W (amateur) 1924. Scored 3 and 4 in only match.

Was a major in the Army.

MARTIN, Evelyn George – RHB RF

b. Upton-on-Severn, 22 March 1881; d. Hadleigh, Suffolk, 27 April 1945. Educated at Eton and New College, Oxford U.

Debut 1903 v Som., Worcester. 3 matches for W 1903–07 (amateur). Highest score: W 18* v Oxford U, Oxford 1907. Best bowling: W 2–73 v Som., Worcester 1903 (on debut).

26 matches Oxford U, 1903–06 – Blue each season. Highest first-class score: 56 Oxford U v Cambridge U, Lord's 1906. Best first-class bowling: 7–81 v Kent, Oxford 1905. 519 runs (12.65) and 107 wickets (23.51) in first-class career.

J.F. Maclean

S.H. Martin

G.T. Mills

MARTIN, Sidney Hugh – RHB LM

b. Durban, S. Africa, 11 January 1909; d. South Africa, February 1988.

Debut 1931 v New Zealand, Worcester. 236 matches for W (professional) 1931–39. Highest score: W 191* v Northants, Worcester 1935. Best bowling: W 8–24 v Sussex, Worcester 1939. 1000 runs (6) 1705 (31.57) 1935 best. 100 wickets (2) – 114 (20.25) 1937 best. 'Double' (2) 1130 runs (21.73) 114 wkts (20.25) 1937. 1262 runs (25.24); 106 wkts (25.00) 1939.

Played for Natal 1925/26–1946/47; Rhodesia 1947/48–1949/50. First-class record: 11491 runs (26.97); 532 wickets (28.31).

Nephew Hugh Tayfield played S. Africa.

MAXWELL, Cecil Reginald Napp – RHB WK

b. London, 21 May 1913; d. Taunton, Som., 25 September 1973. Educated at Brighton College.

Debut 1948 v Notts., Trent Bridge. 7 matches for W 1948–51 (amateur). Highest score: W 31 v Notts., Stourbridge 1949.

Played 16 matches Notts., 1936–39 (cap 1937) and 4 matches Middx. 1946. Also Sir Julien Cahn's Team 1932 to 1938/39. Highest first-class score 268, Cahn's XI v Leics., Nottingham 1935.

MILLS, George Thomas – RHB WK

b. Redditch, 12 September 1923; d. Bromsgrove, 15 September 1983. Educated at Redditch High School and Birmingham U.

Debut 1953 v Cambridge U, Cambridge. 2 matches for W 1953 (amateur). Highest score: 23 v Cambridge U, Cambridge 1953 (on debut).

Birmingham League cricket for Stourbridge. Captained Birmingham U to UAU Trophy 1950.

MITCHELL, Kenneth James – LHB
b. Old Hill, Staffs., 5 December 1924.

Debut 1946 v Notts., Worcester. 1 match for W (amateur) 1946. Scored 10 and 0 in only match.

Birmingham League cricket for Old Hill.

MOORES, Peter – RHB WK
b. Macclesfield, Ches., 18 December 1962. Educated at King Edward VI School, Macclesfield.

Debut 1983 v Som., Worcester. 11 matches for W 1983–84.

55 matches for Sussex since 1985. 1 match Orange Free State 1988/89. Highest score: W 45 v Som., Weston-super-Mare 1984. Highest first-class score: 116 Sussex v Som., Hove 1989. Birmingham League cricket for Dudley.

MORRIS, P.J. – Hard hitting RHB
b. Evesham.

Debut 1914 v Leics., Coalville. 1 match for W (amateur) 1914. 3 and 71 in only match.

Was a bank clerk at his native place.

MORRIS, Raymond – RHB WK
b. Hartlebury, 20 June 1929. Educated at Queen Elizabeth Grammar School, Hartlebury.

P. Moores

H.G. Moule

Debut 1958 v Derby., Kidderminster. 2 matches for W 1958 (amateur). Highest score: W 7 v Leics., Worcester 1958.
Birmingham League cricket for Kidderminster.
Hockey for W.

MORTIMER, Harry – B WK
b. Sculcoates, Yorks., 1872; d. Birmingham, 1953.
Debut 1904 v Kent, Worcester. 1 match for W (professional) 1904.
Scoreboard operator at War. CCC Ground, Edgbaston until death.

MOSS, Reginald Heber – RHB RF/RM
b. Huyton, Lancs., 24 February 1868; d. Bridport, Dorset, 19 March 1956. Educated at Radley and Keble College, Oxford U.
Debut 1925 v Glos., Worcester. 1 match for W (amateur) 1925. Scored 2 and 0 and took 1–5 in only match.
Played 13 matches for Oxford U 1887, 1889, 1890 (Blue 1889). 1 match for Liverpool and District 1893. Highest first-class score: 18* Oxford U v Surrey, Oxford 1887. Best first-class bowling: 4–9 Oxford U v Sussex, Hove 1890. 25 wkts (35.44) in first-class career.
Played only game for W while a local vicar nearly 32 years after previous first-class match in 1893! This is a record gap between two first-class appearances.

MOULE, Harry George – RHB
b. Kidderminster, 23 December 1921.
Debut 1952 v Cambridge U, Worcester. 1 match for W (amateur) 1952. Scored 57 and 45 in only first-class match.
Birmingham League cricket for Kidderminster and Old Hill.

MUNN, Reginald George – RHB

b. Madresfield, 20 August 1869; d. Virginia Water, Surrey, 12 April 1947. Educated at Haileybury.

Debut 1900 v MCC, Lord's. 1 match for W (amateur) 1900. Scored 2 in only innings.

A Regular Army officer.

MURRAY WILLIS, Peter Earnshaw – RHB

b. Castle Bromwich, War., 14 July 1910. Educated at St George's, Harpenden.

Debut 1935 v Lancs., Old Trafford. 7 matches for W (amateur) 1935–36. Highest score: W 20 v War., Worcester 1935.

22 matches Northants (amateur) 1938–46. Cap 1946, captain 1946. Highest first-class score: 54, Northants v W, Kidderminster 1946. Birmingham League cricket for Walsall. Also played for Barnt Green CC.

N

NADEN, James Rupert – RHB RFM
b. Tipton, Staffs, 13 July 1889; d. Sedgley, W, 14 June 1963.
  Debut 1922 v Kent, Kidderminster. 2 matches for W (amateur) 1922.
Highest score: W 16* v Kent, Kidderminster 1922 (debut). Best bowling:
W 2–111 same match.
  Birmingham League cricket for Dudley.

NEALE, Philip Anthony – RHB
b. Scunthorpe, Lincs., 5 June 1954. Educated at Frederick Gough
Grammar School, Scunthorpe and Leeds U.
  Debut 1975 v Surrey, Worcester. 314 matches for W 1975–date. Cap
1978; captain 1982–date; benefit 1988. Highest score: W 167 v Sussex,
Kidderminster 1988. 1000 runs (8) – 1706 (47.39) 1984 best.
  Minor Counties cricket Lincs., 1972.
  Played soccer for Lincoln City.

P.A. Neale

J.R. Naden

Phil Neale holds aloft the Refuge Sunday League Trophy.

NESBITT, Arnold Stearns – RHB WK
b. Chertsey, Surrey, 16 October 1878; d. in action, Ploegsteert Wood, Belgium, 7 November 1914. Educated at Bradfield.
 ·Debut 1914 v Middx., Lord's. 1 match for W (amateur) 1914. Scored 3 and 2* in only match.

NESFIELD, Edward Roy – RHB OB
b. Armthorpe, Yorks., 7 March 1900. Educated at King's School, Worcester.

Debut 1919 v H.K. Foster's XI, Hereford. 3 matches for W (amateur) 1919–20. Highest score: 16 v H.K. Foster's XI, Hereford 1919 (on debut).

NEVILE, Bernard Philip – RHB RF
b. Wellingore, Lincs., 1 August 1888; d. in action, Ypres, Belgium, 11 February 1916. Educated at Downside and Cambridge U.

Debut 1913 v Middx., Worcester. 5 matches for W (amateur) 1913. Highest score: W 17* v Kent, Tunbridge Wells 1913. Best bowling: W 4–53 v Surrey, The Oval 1913.

Played Minor Counties for Lincs., 1911–13.

NEWPORT, Philip John – RHB RFM
b. High Wycombe, Bucks, 11 October 1962. Educated at High Wycombe Royal Grammar School and Portsmouth Polytechnic.

Debut 1982 v Pakistan, Worcester. 111 matches for W 1982–date. Highest score: W 77* v Yorks., Worcester 1988. Best bowling: W 8–52 v Middx., Lord's 1988. Shares W 7th wicket record stand – 205 with G.A. Hick v Yorks., Worcester 1988.

2 tests for England 1988–89. Highest score: 26 v Sri Lanka, Lord's 1988. Best test bowling: 4–87 same match. Played Boland (S. Africa) 1987/88; highest first-class score: 86, Boland v Transvaal B, Stellenbosch 1987/88. Played Bucks in Minor Counties Championship 1981–82. Birmingham League cricket for Worcester City.

P.J. Newport

E.W. Norton

M. Nichol

NICHOL, Maurice – RHB

b. Hetton-le-Hole, Co. Durham, 10 September 1904; d. Chelmsford, Essex, 21 May 1934. (Was found dead in his hotel on second morning of match, W v Essex, Chelmsford.)

Debut 1928 v W. Indies, Worcester. 135 matches for W (professional) 1928–34. Highest score: W 262* v Hants, Bournemouth 1930. 1000 runs (4) – 2154 (43.95) 1933 best. Scored 8 centuries 1933. Scored 104 on debut v W. Indies in 1928.

Played Durham in Minor Counties 1923–28.

NICHOLS, John Ernest – B

b. Acle, nr Norwich, 20 April 1878; d. Thorpe, Norwich, 29 February 1952.

Debut 1902 v Sussex, Worcester. 5 matches for W 1902–04 (professional). Highest score: W 13 v Yorks., Sheffield 1904.

1 first-class match for Minor Counties v South Africa, Stoke-on-Trent 1912. Birmingham League cricket for West Bromwich Dartmouth and Stourbridge. Minor Counties cricket for Staffs. 1907–14; Norfolk 1921.

NORTON, Ernest Wilmott – RHB LBG

b. Sparkhill, Birmingham, 19 June 1889; d. Birmingham, April 1972. Educated at King Edwards Grammar School, Camp Hill, Birmingham.

Debut 1922 v Som., Worcester. 6 matches for W (amateur) 1922–23. Highest score: W 23 v Glos., Worcester 1922. Best bowling: W 3–74 v Glos., Worcester 1922.

2 matches for War. 1920 as amateur. Highest first-class score: 26* War. v Leics., Edgbaston 1920. Club cricket for Harborne, Knowle and Dorridge and King's Heath.

Ian Botham and Phil Newport celebrate with a bottle of champagne.

OAKLEY, Leonard – LHB SLA
b. Stourbridge, W 11 January 1916.

Debut 1935 v Middx., Worcester. 8 matches for W 1935–48 (professional). Highest score: W 11 v Lancs., Old Trafford 1948. Best bowling: W 6–64 v RAF, Worcester 1946.

Birmingham League cricket for West Bromwich Dartmouth.

ORMROD, Joseph Alan – RHB OB
b. Ramsbottom, Lancs., 22 December 1942. Educated at Kirkcaldy High School, Fife, Scotland.

Debut 1962 v Lancs., Stourbridge. 465 matches for W 1962–83, commencing as professional. Cap 1966; benefit (£19,000) 1977. Highest score: W 204* v Kent, Dartford 1973. Best bowling: W 5–27 v Glos.,

J.A. Ormrod

L. Oakley

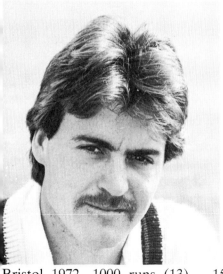

L. Outschoorn

S.J. O'Shaughnessy

Bristol 1972. 1000 runs (13) – 1535 (45.14) 1978 best. Carried bat throughout innings 4 times; 66*/187 v Essex, Chelmsford 1975; 36*/73 v Sussex, Worcester 1977; 126*/219 v Hants, Bournemouth 1980; 63*/136 v Derby., Derby 1983. 101 and 131* in match v Som., Worcester 1980. Added 291 for 1st wicket with G.M. Turner v War., Worcester 1982. Best W 1st wicket stand since 1913. Record 4th wicket stand – 281 with Younis Ahmed v Notts., Trent Bridge 1979. 384 first-class catches for W – 2nd best for County.
      Played Lancs., 1984–85 – cap 1984. Now on coaching staff. Birmingham League cricket Stourbridge and Dudley.

O'SHAUGHNESSY, Steven Joseph – RHB RM
b. Bury, Lancs., 9 September 1961. Educated at Harper Green Secondary School, Farnworth.
      Debut 1988 v Notts., Worcester. 11 matches for W 1988–89. Highest score: W 44 v Notts., Worcester 1988 (debut). Best bowling: W 2–55 v Leics., Leicester 1988.
      100 matches Lancs., 1980–87 (cap 1985). Highest first-class score: 159* Lancs. v Somerset, Bath 1984. Best first-class bowling: 4–66 Lancs. v Notts., Trent Bridge 1982. 100 in 35 minutes, Lancs. v Leics., Old Trafford 1983, when fed easy bowling in attempt to encourage declaration. Equalled world record held by P.G.H. Fender. Century in 25 scoring strokes a new world record. 1167 runs (34.32) in 1984. Birmingham League cricket for West Bromwich Dartmouth.

OUTSCHOORN, Ladislaw ('Laddie') – RHB RM
b. Colombo, Ceylon (now Sri Lanka), 26 September 1918.
      Debut 1946 v Combined Services, Worcester. 341 matches for W

1946–59 (professional). Cap 1948; benefit (£3,540) 1959. Highest score: W 215* v Northants, Worcester 1949. Best bowling: W 2–15 v Lancs., Blackpool 1953. 1000 runs (9) – 1761 (35.93) 1951 best. 5 catches in innings v Derby., Kidderminster 1948 – equalled W record at the time. 55 catches in 1949 created W record, subsequently beaten only by D.W. Richardson in 1961. Also 43 catches in 1951, placing him second at the time. 276 catches in career – 6th for county.

Birmingham League cricket Kidderminster and West Bromwich Dartmouth. Formerly Sri Lanka National coach; played for Singapore pre-1940.

PALMER, Cecil Howard – RHB

b. Eastbourne, Sussex, 14 July 1873; d. in action, at Gallipoli, 26 July 1915. Educated at Radley.

Debut 1904 v Oxford U, Worcester. 1 match for W (amateur) 1904. 41 and 75* in only match. 8 matches Hants 1899–1907 (amateur). 380 first-class runs (23.75).

Regular Army officer whose appearance were restricted. Unique in playing first-class matches for and against W at Worcester in the same season (1904).

PALMER, Charles Henry – RHB RM or RAS 'donkey drops'.

b. Old Hill, Staffs., 15 May 1919. Educated at Halesowen Grammar School and Birmingham U.

Charles H. Palmer

M.F.W. Passey

J.M. Parker

Debut 1938 v Yorks., Bradford. 66 matches for W 1938–49 (amateur). Highest score: W 177 v Notts., Dudley 1947. Best bowling: W 4–50 v Yorks., Worcester 1948.

231 matches Leics., 1950–59. Captain 1950–57; cap 1950. Highest score first-class: 201 Leics. v Northants, Northampton 1953. Best first-class bowling: 8–7 Leics. v Surrey, Leicester 1955. 2071 runs (39.82) in 1952. 1 test for England v W. Indies, 1953/54 while player-manager of MCC party. Highest test score 22. Birmingham League cricket for Old Hill. 17458 first-class runs (31.74); 365 wickets (25.15).

Leics. secretary 1950–57; current Chairman Leics. CCC. MCC President 1978/79.

PARKER, John Morton – RHB LBG occ WK
b. Dannevirke, Hawkes Bay, New Zealand, 21 February 1951. Educated at Mahura ngi College, Warkworth, New Zealand.

Debut 1971 v India, Worcester. 61 matches for W 1971–75. Cap 1974. Highest score: W 140 v Essex, Worcester 1974. Best bowling: W 3–26 v Oxford U, Worcester 1975. 75 matches for Northern Districts (New Zealand) 1972/73–83/84.

Highest first-class score: 195, N. Districts v Canterbury, Whangarei 1972/73. 36 tests for New Zealand 1972/73–80/81. Highest test score: 121 v England, Auckland 1974/75. 1498 test runs (24.55). First-class runs 11254 (34.84). Birmingham League cricket for Kidderminster.

PASSEY, Michael Francis William – RHB OB
b. Crossway Green, 6 June 1937.

Debut 1953 v Glam., Worcester (aged 16). 1 match for W 1953 as professional. 1 run in only innings; 1–57 in only innings bowled in.

PATAUDI, Nawab of (Iftiqar Ali Khan) –
b. Pataudi, Punjab, India, 16 March 1910; d. New Delhi, India, 5 January 1952. Educated at Chief's College, Lahore; Balliol College, Oxford U.

Debut 1932 v India, Worcester. 37 matches for W 1932–38 (amateur); capped. Highest score: W 231* v Essex, Worcester 1933. Also scored 224* W v Kent, Worcester 1933; 222 W v Som., Weston 1933; 214* W v Glam., Worcester 1934.

35 matches for Oxford U, 1928–31; Blue 1929–31. Scored 238* (highest first-class score) v Cambridge U, Lord's 1931 – still record for Oxbridge match. Scored 1582 runs (51.03) W 1933. Played Indian domestic cricket for Patiala, N. Indian States and S. Punjab, 1931/32–45/46. Captained India in England 1946. 3 tests for England v Australia 1932/33–1934. 3 tests for India 1946. 199 test runs (19.90). Highest test score: 102 England v Australia, Sydney 1932/33 (test debut). 8750 first-class runs (48.61); 15 wickets (35.26). Best first-class bowling 6–111, Viceroy's XI v Roshanara, Delhi 1931/32.

Son Mansur Ali (Sussex, Oxford U and India).

PATEL, Dipak Narshibhai – RHB OB
b. Nairobi, Kenya, 25 October 1958. Educated at George Salter School, West Bromwich.

Debut 1976 v War., Worcester. 234 matches for W 1976–86. Cap 1979. Highest score: W 197 v Cambridge U, Worcester 1984. Best bowling: W

D.N. Patel

Nawab of Pataudi

Nawab of Pataudi 1932–38

7–46 v Lancs., Worcester 1982. 1000 runs (6) – 1615 (38.45) 1983 best. Set County 6th wicket record of 227 with E.J.O. Hemsley v Oxford U, Oxford 1976 – lasted until 1988.

Plays Auckland (New Zealand). 7 tests for New Zealand since 1986/87; 267 runs (19.07); 0 wickets. Birmingham League cricket for West Bromwich Dartmouth and Dudley. Minor Counties for Staffs. 1987.

PATEL, Harshad Vallabhbhia – RHB
b. Nairobi, Kenya, 29 January 1964. Educated at George Salter High School, West Bromwich; Rowley Regis College.

Debut 1985 v Cambridge U, Cambridge. 1 match for W 1985. Scored 39 in only innings.

Birmingham League cricket Stourbridge and West Bromwich Dartmouth. Plays Staffs., in Birmingham League.

Cousin Dipak Patel (W and New Zealand).

PAWSON, Albert Guy – RHB WK
b. Bramley, Yorks., 30 May 1888; d. Lamerton, Devon, 25 February 1986. Educated at Winchester and Christchurch College, Oxford U.

Debut 1908 v Oxford U, Oxford. 1 match for W (amateur) 1908. Scored 0* and 12 in only match; stumped 3 batsmen in first innings.

26 matches Oxford U 1908–11. Blue each season. Highest first-class score 41*, Oxford U v Gents of England, Oxford 1908.

Brother A.C. Pawson (Oxford U); son H.A. Pawson (Kent and Oxford U).

H.V. Patel

A.G. Pawson

D.B. Pearson   *F.A. Pearson*

PEARSON, Derek Brook – RHB RFM
b. Stourbridge, 29 March 1937.

Debut 1954 v Cambridge U, Worcester. 74 matches for W
(professional) 1954–61. Cap 1959. Highest score: W 49 v Glos., Stroud
1959. Best bowling: W 6–70 v Leics., Leicester 1959. No-balled for
throwing 1954, 1959, 1960.

Birmingham League cricket for Stourbridge, West Bromwich
Dartmouth, Dudley.

PEARSON, Frederick Albert – RHB OB/LB
b. Brixton, London, 23 September 1880; d. Droitwich, 10 November
1963.

Debut 1900 v London County, Worcester. 445 matches for W 1900–26
(professional). Highest score: W 167 v Glam., Swansea 1921. Best
bowling: W 8–97 v Hants, Bournemouth 1921. 1000 runs (6) – 1498
(36.53) 1921 best. 111 wickets (22.89) 1923 – also 1052 runs (25.04) and
'double'.

Best first-class bowling 9–41, H.K. Foster's XI v Oxford U, Oxford
1914.

PERKS, Reginald Thomas David – LHB RFM
b. Hereford, 4 October 1911; d. Worcester, 22 November 1977.

Debut 1930 v Surrey, The Oval. 561 matches for W 1930–55
(professional). Cap 1931; benefit (£3,000) 1947; testimonial (£2,600)

1955; captain 1955. Highest score: W 75 v Notts., Trent Bridge 1938. Best bowling: W 9–40 v Glam., Stourbridge 1939. 100 wickets (15) (W record) – 154 (18.83) 1939 best. Match figures of 15–106, v Essex, Worcester 1937. Hat tricks v Kent, Stourbridge 1931, and v War., Edgbaston 1933. 2143 wickets (23.73) County record.

2 tests for England 1938/39–39. Best test bowling 5–100 v S. Africa, Durban 1938/39. 2233 first-class wickets (24.07). Played Birmingham League cricket for Dudley, West Bromwich Dartmouth and Kidderminster.

Father Tom Perks was well-known groundsman; 1 first-class match for MCC 1902.

PERRY, Ernest Harvey – RHB RFM
b. Chaddesley Corbett, 16 January 1908.

Debut 1946 v War., Edgbaston. 10 matches for W 1933–46 (amateur). Highest score: W 46 v Glam., Dudley 1946. Best bowling: W 5–42 v Leics., Kidderminster 1933.

Birmingham League cricket for Kidderminster.

E.H. Perry

R.T.D. Perks

H. Perry

S.P. Perryman

PERRY, Harry – RHB RM

b. Stourbridge, 1895; d. Stourbridge, 28 February 1961.

Debut 1927 v Som., Stourbridge. 5 matches for W (amateur) 1927–28. Highest score: W 40 v Yorks., Worcester 1927. Best bowling: 1–38 v Hants, Worcs 1928.

Birmingham League cricket for Stourbridge.

PERRYMAN, Stephen Peter – RHB RM

b. Yardley, Birmingham, 22 October 1955. Educated at Sheldon Heath Comprehensive.

Debut 1982 v Oxford U, Oxford. 25 matches for W 1982–83. Highest score: W 22 v Leics., Hereford 1983. Best bowling: W 6–49 v Lancs. Blackpool 1982.

131 matches for War. 1974–81 (cap 1977). Highest first-class score: 43 War. v Som., Edgbaston 1977. Best first-class bowling: 7–49 War. v Hants, Bournemouth 1978. 358 first-class wickets (31.66). Birmingham League cricket for Mitchells & Butlers. Played Staffs. (Minor Counties Championship) 1988.

PHELPS, Peter Horsley – RHB

b. Malvern, 5 February 1909. Educated at Felsted.

Debut 1931 v Northants, Northampton. 3 matches for W (amateur) 1931–32. Highest score: W 11 v Leics., Worcester 1931.

PONSONBY, Cecil Brabazon – RHB WK
b. London, 26 December 1892; d. St John's Wood, London, 11 May 1945. Educated at Eton and Pembroke College, Oxford U.
  Debut 1911 v Leics., Worcester. 74 matches for W 1911–28 (amateur). Captain 1927. Highest score: W 50* v Surrey, the Oval 1912.

PORTHOUSE, Stanley Clive – RHB
b. Redditch, 14 August 1910.
  Debut 1934 v Yorks., Worcester. 5 matches for W (amateur) 1934–35. Highest score: W 27 v Yorks., Worcester 1934 (on debut).

POWELL, Albert James – RHB RM
b. Presteigne, Radnorshire, 8 December 1893; d. Liskeard, Cornwall, 15 February 1979.
  Debut 1921 v Lancs., Worcester. 1 match for W 1921 (amateur). Scored 9 and 1 in only match.

A.J. Powell

C.B. Ponsonby

H.J. Powys-Keck

C.R. Preece

POWYS-KECK, Horatio James – LFM

b. in Switzerland, 8 March 1873; d. Kensington, London, 30 January 1952. Educated at Malvern, Monkton Combe and Oxford U.

Debut 1903 v Hants, Southampton. Highest score: W 25 v Hants, Southampton 1903 (debut). Best bowling: 2–65 same match.

Toured India with Oxford Authentics in 1902/03 and W. Indies with Lord Brackley's team in 1904/05.

An Army officer.

PRATT, David – RHB SLA

b. Watford, Herts, 20 July 1938.

Debut 1959 v Derby., Chesterfield. 8 matches for W (professional) 1959. Highest score: W 3* v Derby., Worcester 1959. Best bowling: W 5–54 v Surrey, Worcester 1959.

3 matches for Services 1961; 7 matches for Notts. 1962. Highest first-class score: 14, Services v S. African Fezela, Portsmouth 1961. Minor Counties Championship for Herts., 1957. Birmingham League cricket for Stourbridge.

PREECE, Charles Richard – RHB RMF

b. Broad Heath, 15 December 1887; d. Oldbury, 5 February 1976.

Debut 1920 v Hants, Worcester. 88 matches for W 1920–27 (professional). Highest score: W 69 v Sussex, Worcester 1922. Best bowling: W 7–35 v Essex, Leyton 1921. Hat trick v War., Edgbaston 1924.

J. Price

A.P. Pridgeon

PRICE, John – RHB RFM
b. Worcester, 6 July 1908.
    Debut 1927 v New Zealand, Worcester. 11 matches for W (amateur) 1927–29. Highest score: W 33 v Derby., Kidderminster 1928. Best bowling: W 2–35 v Som., Stourbridge 1927.
    Brother W.H. Price (W).

PRICE, William Harry – RHB RFM
b. Worcester, 28 May 1900; d. Worcester, 15 April 1982. Educated at Worcester Royal Grammar School.
    Debut 1923 v Glam., Cardiff. 1 match for W (amateur) 1923. 0 runs, 0 wkts.
    Brother J. Price (W).

PRICE, Walter Longsdon – LHB LM
b. Toxteth Park, Liverpool, 2 February 1886; d. Lechlade, Glos., 26 December 1943. Educated at Repton.
    Debut 1904 v Oxford U, Worcester. 3 matches for W (amateur) 1904. Highest score: W 7 v Hants, Worcester 1904. Best bowling: W 4–86 v Surrey, Worcester 1904.
    Represented Canada in 1912.

PRIDGEON, Anthony Paul – RHB RMF
b. Wall Heath, Staffs., 22 February 1954. Educated at Summerhill

C.D.A. Pullan

Secondary School, Kingswinford.

Debut 1972 v Cambridge U, Cambridge. 240 matches for W 1972–89. Cap 1980; benefit 1989. Highest score: W 67 v War., Worcester 1984. Best bowling: W 7–35 v Oxford U, Oxford 1976.

Birmingham League cricket at various times for Stourbridge, Moseley, Dudley, Duport and Kidderminster.

PULLAN, Cecil Douglas Ayrton – RHB RMF
b. Mahoba, India, 26 July 1910; d. Tongaat Beech, Natal, S. Africa, 24 June 1970. Educated at Malvern and Trinity College, Oxford U.

Debut 1935 v Middx., Lord's. 35 matches for W (amateur) 1935–38. Highest score: W 84 v Glos., Cheltenham 1938. Best bowling: W 2–26 v Surrey, the Oval 1938.

6 matches Oxford U 1932–33 (no Blue).

Won a Blue for boxing.

QUAIFE, Bernard William – RHB WK RAB
b. Olton, Solihull, War., 24 November 1899; d. Bridport, Dorset, 27 November 1984. Educated at Solihull Grammar School.

Debut 1928 v Sussex, Worcester. 271 matches for W 1928–37 (amateur). Capped. Highest score: W 136* v Leics., Worcester 1928. Best bowling: W 2–5 v Leics., Leicester 1934. 1000 runs (2) – 1167 (26.52) 1935 best. Added 277 with H.H.I.H. Gibbons v Middx., Worcester 1931 – 4th wicket record until 1979.

48 matches for War. 1920–26 (capped). 9594 first-class runs (20.02); 186 catches, 54 stumpings as wicketkeeper. Local club cricket for Olton.

Father W.G. Quaife (War., and England); uncle W. Quaife (Sussex and War.).

B.W. Quaife

R

RADFORD, Neal Victor – RHB RFM
b. Luanshya, N. Rhodesia (now Zambia), 7 June 1957. Educated at Athlone High School, Jo'burg.

Debut 1985 v Middx., Lord's. 106 matches for W 1985–date. Cap 1985. Highest score: W 66* v Sussex, Hove 1989. Best bowling: W 9–70 v Som., Worcester 1986.

24 matches Lancs., 1980–84. Plays Transvaal in Currie Cup. 3 tests for England 1986–87/88. 4 wickets (87.75). Highest first-class score: 76* Lancs. v Derby., Blackpool 1981. 2604 first-class runs (16.07); 775 wickets (24.72). Played Lancashire league cricket for Burnley, Bacup and Nelson.

Brother W.R. Radford (Orange Free State).

RHODES, Steven John – RHB WK
b. Bradford, 17 June 1964. Educated at Lapage Middle School; Carlton-Bolling School, Bradford.

N.V. Radford

S.J. Rhodes

D.W. Richardson   *P.E. Richardson*

Debut 1985 v Middx., Lord's. 120 matches for W 1985–date. Cap 1986. Highest score: W 108 v Derby., Derby 1988. Twice achieved 6 wicket-keeping dismissals in innings, equalling county record for championship matches: v Sussex, Kidderminster 1988 and v War., Edgbaston 1989 (all caught each time). 9 dismissals in match (all ct) v Sussex, Kidderminster in 1988, equalling county record of H. Yarnold. Shares county 6th wicket record stand with G.A. Hick – 265 v Som., Taunton 1988.

3 matches for Yorks., 1981–84. Toured Sri Lanka 1985/86 and Zimbabwe 1989/90 with England 'B'. Represented England in Texaco Trophy v Australia 1989.

Father W.E. Rhodes (Notts.).

RICHARDSON, Derek Walter ('Dick') – LHB LM
b. Hereford, 3 November 1934. Educated at Hereford Cathedral School.

Debut 1952 v Oxford U, Oxford. 371 matches for W (originally amateur – professional from 1956) 1952–67. Cap 1956; benefit 1967. Highest score: W 169 v Derby., Dudley 1957. Best bowling: W 2–11 v Lancs., Old Trafford 1963. 1000 runs (8) – 1825 (36.50) 1962 best. Club record 65 catches in 1961; also 51 in 1964, 42 1962, 41 1963. Career total of 414 catches club record.

1 test, England v W. Indies, Trent Bridge 1957; 33 in only innings.

Brothers P.E. (W, Kent and England) and B.A, (War.) Richardson. Birmingham League cricket for Stourbridge and Old Hill.

RICHARDSON, Peter Edward – LHB
b. Hereford, 4 July 1931. Educated at Hereford Cathedral School.

Debut 1949 v Cambridge U, Worcester. 161 matches for W (amateur) 1949–58. Cap 1952; captain 1956–58. Highest score: W 185 v Som., Kidderminster 1954. 1000 runs (5) 2029 (39.01) 1953 best. Carried bat through innings 91*/155 v Hants, Worcester 1955. W joint-secretary 1956–57.

Played 162 matches for Kent 1959–65, starting as professional. Cap 1960, benefit 1965. 34 tests for England 1956–63. 2061 runs (37.47). Highest test score: 126 v W. Indies, Trent Bridge 1957. On committee of Kent CCC from 1979. Birmingham League cricket for Stourbridge.

Brothers D.W. (W and England) and B.A. (War.) Richardson.

RICHARDSON, William Ethelbert – RHB RF

b. St Helens, Lancs., 23 December 1894; d. Hartlebury, 5 November 1971.

Debut 1920 v Hants, Worcester. 30 matches for W (amateur) 1920–28. Highest score: W 24 v War., Stourbridge 1922. Best bowling: W 6–48 v Glos., Gloucester 1920.

Birmingham League cricket for Kidderminster. Top class Rugby Union football for Moseley.

RIGHTON, Edward Grantham Jnr – RHB

b. Evesham, 24 September 1912; d. Evesham, 2 May 1986. Educated at Dean Close School, Cheltenham.

Debut 1934 v War., Kidderminster. 4 matches for W (amateur) 1934–36. Highest score: W 19 v Derby., Chesterfield 1936.

Father E.G. Righton Snr (W).

E.G. Righton Jnr

W.E. Richardson

J. Riley

RIGHTON, Edward Grantham Snr – RHB RM
b. Evesham, 23 November 1885; d. Evesham, 3 January 1964. Educated at Dean Close School, Cheltenham.
Debut 1911 v Leics., Worcester. 4 matches for W (amateur) 1911–13. Highest score: W 48 v Leics., Worcester on debut.
Son E.G. Righton Jnr (W).

RILEY, Jack – RHB SLA
b. Accrington, Lancs., 27 April 1927. Educated at All Saints School, Clayton-le-Moors.
Debut 1953 v Cambridge U, Cambridge. 1 match for W 1953 as professional. 1 run in only innings. Best bowling W 3–25 in same match.
Lancs cricket for Enfield and Great Harwood.

ROBERTS, Christopher Paul – RHB RM
b. Cleethorpes, Lincs., 12 October 1951; d. in climbing accident, Coombe Ghyl, Borrowdale, Cumberland, 9 June 1977. Educated at Humberston Foundation School, Cleethorpes; Borough Road College of Education, Isleworth.
Debut 1974 v Glam., Worcester. No runs or wkts in only match.
Played Lincs. in Minor Counties Championship 1971–72.

ROBERTS, Edward Stanley – B
b. Oswestry, Shrops., 6 May 1890; d. in Rhodesia, September 1964.
Debut 1925 v Som., Worcester. 3 matches for W (amateur) 1925. Highest score: W 12 v Derby., Stourbridge 1925.

ROBINSON, A.W. – B
Debut 1920 v Hants, Worcester. 6 matches for W (amateur) 1920–26.
Highest score: W 37 v Yorks., Harrogate 1925.

ROBINSON, Peter James – LHB SLA
b. Worcester, 9 February 1943.
  Debut 1963 v Pakistan Eaglets, Worcester. 5 matches for W 1963–64.
Highest score: W 37 v Hants, Bournemouth 1963. Best bowling: W 2–12
v Cambridge U, Halesowen 1964.
  180 matches Som., 1965–77. Cap 1966. Highest first-class score: 140
Som. v Northants, Northampton 1970. Best first-class bowling: 7–10
Som. v Notts., Trent Bridge 1966. 1158 runs (26.93) 1970. Birmingham
League cricket for Kidderminster and Stourbridge.
  Appointed groundsman-coach to Somerset after retirement. Uncle
Roly Jenkins (W and England).

ROBSON, Clayton Graeme Wynne – RHB
b. Bareilly, India, 3 July 1901; d. Long Melford, Suffolk, 26 February
1989. Educated at Malvern and Sandhurst RMC.
  Debut 1921 v Hants, Worcester 1921. 2 matches for W (amateur) 1921.
Highest score 46 W v Hants, Worcester 1921 on debut.
  4 matches Middx. (amateur) 1926.

A.W. Robinson

P.J. Robinson

C.F. Root

H.O. Rogers

ROGERS, Harry Oliver – LHB RFM
b. Hednesford, Staffs., 21 January 1889; d. Worcester, 4 July 1956.
    Debut 1923 v Glos., Worcester. 86 matches for W (professional)
1923–28. Highest score: W 118* v Sussex, Stourbridge 1925. Best
bowling: W 8–85 v Yorks., Worcester 1925.

ROMNEY, Francis William – RHB
b. Tewkesbury, Glos., 25 November 1873; d. Malvern, 28 January 1963.
Educated at Malvern.
    Debut 1900 v Leics., Leicester. 4 matches for W (amateur) 1900.
Highest score: W 20* v Oxford U, Oxford 1900.

ROOT, Charles Frederick – RHB RFM/M
b. Somercotes, Derby., 16 April 1890; d. Wolverhampton, 20 January
1954.
    Debut 1921 v Lancs., Old Trafford. 284 matches for W (professional)
1921–32. Capped. Highest score: W 107 v Kent, Worcester 1928. Best

bowling: W 9–23 v Lancs., Worcester 1921. Also 9–40 v Essex, Worcester 1924; 9–81 v Kent, Tunbridge Wells 1930. 100 wickets (9) 207 (17.52) 1925 best (W record). 'Double' 1928 – 1044 runs (20.88); 118 wickets (29.66).

57 matches for Derby. 1910–20. 3 tests for England 1926 8 wickets for 194 runs. First-class record: 7911 runs (14.78); 243 ct; 1512 wkts (21.11). Birmingham League cricket for Dudley.

Autobiography *A Cricket Pro's Lot* (1937); for many years cricket writer for *Sunday Pictorial*.

ROSE, Thomas Ginnever – LHB SLA
b. Ilkeston, Derby., 16 March 1901; d. St Ives, Cornwall, 8 August 1979.

Debut 1922 v Sussex, Hove. 6 matches for W 1922 (professional). Highest score: W 15 v Sussex, Hove 1922 (on debut). Best bowling: W 3–68 v Kent, Gravesend 1922.

RUDGE, Lloyd Maurice – RHB RFM
b. Walsall, Staffs., 11 February 1934.

Debut 1952 v Combined Services, Worcester. 1 match for W (amateur) 1952. 1 run in only innings: 0 wickets.

Three great England players chatting. Left to right: Wilf Rhodes, Roly Jenkins and Sid Barnes.

F.E. Rumsey

I.A. Rutherford

RUMSEY, Frederick Edward – RHB LFM
b. Stepney, London, 4 December 1935. Educated at Coopers' Co. School, London.

Debut 1960 v Cambridge U, Worcester. 13 matches for W 1960–62 (professional). Highest score: W 43 v Sussex, Worcester 1960. Best bowling: W 7–50 v Derby., Chesterfield 1962 (11–96 match).

153 matches Som., 1963–68 (Cap 1963). 1 match for Derby. 1970. 5 tests for England 1964–65; 17 wickets (27.11). Highest first-class score: 45, Som. v Sussex, Weston-super-Mare 1967. Best first-class bowling: 8–26 Som. v Hants, Bath 1965. 1015 first-class runs (8.45); 580 wickets (20.29). Birmingham League cricket for Kidderminster.

PRO for Derby. in 1969; now travel agent specializing in trips abroad for cricket purposes.

RUTHERFORD, Ian Alexander – RHB RM
b. Dunedin, New Zealand, 30 June 1957; Educated at King's High School, Dunedin.

Debut 1976 v Oxford U, Oxford. 2 matches for W 1976. Highest score: W 8 v W. Indies, Worcester 1976. 1–15 in same match, only wicket.

Played Otago (New Zealand) 1974/75 to 1983/84. Highest first-class score 222 Otago v Central Districts, New Plymouth 1978/79. First-class record: 3794 runs (27.10).

Brother K.R. Rutherford (New Zealand).

Peter Richardson and Don Kenyon, a successful opening partnership, going to the wicket before the Australian match in 1956

Berrow's Newspapers

SALE, Henry George – RHB
b. Shipston-on-Stour, War., 26 March 1889; d. Shipston-on-Stour, 30 August 1975. Educated at Wellingborough.

Debut 1921 v Notts., Trent Bridge. 4 matches for W 1921–25 (amateur). Highest score: W 28* v Northants, Northampton 1925.

SANDERSON, Gerald Barry – RHB
b. Toxteth Park, Liverpool, 12 May 1881; d. Westminster, London, 3 October 1964. Educated at Malvern.

Debut 1923 v Northants, Worcester. 1 match for W 1923 (amateur). Scored 16 in only innings.

1 match for War. 1901 – scored 1 in only innings. Was run out in both first-class innings. Played for Coventry and N. War.

G.B. Sanderson

J.C. Scholey

SANTALL, John Frank Eden – RHB RM
b. King's Heath, Birmingham, 3 December 1907; d. Bournemouth, Hants, May 1986.
   Debut 1930 v Essex, Leyton. 8 matches for W 1930 as professional. Highest score: 36* v Lancs., Worcester 1930. Best bowling: W 2–29 on debut.
   Became professional ice skater and instructor. Father S. Santall and brother F.R. Santall both War.

SAUNDERS, Martyn – RHB RFM
b. Worcester, 16 May 1958. Educated at Worcester Technical College.
   Debut 1980 v Lancs., Stourport. 3 matches for W 1980. Highest score: W 12 v Notts., Worcester 1980. Best bowling: W 3–47 v Kent, Worcester 1980.
   Birmingham League cricket for Stourbridge.

SCHOLEY, John Colin – RHB WK
b. Leeds, Yorks., 28 September 1930. Educated at Leeds Grammar School.
   Debut 1952 v India, Worcester. 10 matches for W 1952–53 (professional). Highest score: W 16 v Kent, Worcester 1952.
   Club cricket in Yorks. for Leeds, Baildon and Undercliffe.

SCOTHERN, Michael Graham – RHB RFM
b. Skipton, Yorks., 9 March 1961.
　Debut 1986 v Cambridge U, Cambridge. 1 match for W 1986. Did not bat: 1–42 in only bowl.
　Plays Cumberland in Minor Counties Championship.

SCOTT, Mark Stephen – RHB
b. Muswell Hill, London, 10 March 1959. Educated at Creighton High School, Muswell Hill.
　Debut 1981 v Surrey, the Oval. 32 matches for W 1981–83. Highest score: W 109 v Glos., Bristol 1981. 968 runs (26.88) in debut season.
　Birmingham League cricket for West Bromwich Dartmouth and Worcester City. Now on county coaching staff.

SEDGLEY, John Brian – RHB
b. West Bromwich, Staffs., 17 February 1939.
　Debut 1959 v Oxford U, Oxford. 15 matches for W 1959–61 (professional). Highest score: W 95 v Derby., Derby 1960.
　Very experienced Birmingham League cricketer, having played for Dudley, Stourbridge, Old Hill, Moseley, and Mitchells & Butlers.

M.S. Scott

J.B. Sedgley

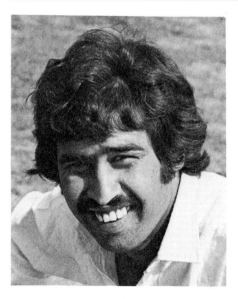

R. Senghera

W.H.N. Shakespeare

SEELEY, Gerald Henry – RHB

b. Port Blair, Andaman Islands, 9 May 1903; d. at sea off Belgian coast, 23 July 1941 (in action). Educated at Marlborough.

Debut 1921 v Notts., Worcester. 1 match for W (amateur) 1921. Scored 7 in only innings.

SENGHERA, Ravindra – RHB OB

b. Delhi, India, 25 January 1947.

Debut 1974 v Cambridge U, Cambridge 1974. 23 matches for W 1974–76. Highest score: W 36* v Glos., Cheltenham 1975. Best bowling: W 5–81 v Oxford U, Oxford 1974.

Birmingham League cricket for Smethwick.

SERRURIER, Louis Roy – RHB RM

b. Cape Town, S. Africa, 7 February 1905. Educated in Cape Town and Brasenose College, Oxford U.

Debut 1927 v Notts., Trent Bridge. 7 matches for W 1927 (amateur). Highest score: W 110 v Glos., Bristol. 1927. Best bowling: W 2–31 v Notts., Trent Bridge 1927.

Played 11 matches for Oxford U 1925–27 without winning Blue. Played in S. Africa for Western Province – 1927/28–1929/30 – and Transvaal – 1931/32. Highest first-class score: 171, Western Province v Eastern Province, Cape Town 1928/29. Best first-class bowling: 5–103 Oxford U v Essex, Chelmsford 1927. 1281 first-class runs (33.71); 42 wickets (26.83).

SHAKESPEARE, William Harold Nelson – RHB

b. Worcester, 24 August 1893. d. Whittington, 10 July 1976. Educated at

Worcester Royal Grammar School.

Debut 1919 v War., Edgbaston. 26 matches for W (amateur) 1919–31. Highest score: W 67* v War., Edgbaston 1919 on debut. At time of death was President of W CCC.

An early member of the AFC, reached the rank of Wing-Commander. While domiciled in London played successfully for Brondesbury.

SHEPHERD, Sydney George – RHB RFM

b. York, 23 August 1908; d. in Cheshire, 20 December 1987.

Debut 1936 v Yorks., Stourbridge. 1 match for W 1936 (professional). Scored 9 and 0 in only match.

Played Minor Counties cricket for Ches. 1946–50. Professional for Bootle CC for many years.

SHEPPARD, Geoffrey Alan – B

b. 18 December 1890; d. Newbury, Berks., 22 May 1940. Educated at Charterhouse.

Debut 1919 v Glos., Worcester. 2 matches for W (amateur) 1919. Highest score: 11 v Glos., Worcester 1919 on debut.

SHEPPARD, Thomas Winter – RHB

b. Havant, Hants, 4 March 1873; d. Callander, Perthshire, 7 June 1954. Educated at Haileybury.

Debut 1909 v Oxford U, Oxford. 1 match for W 1909 (amateur). Scored 22 and 14 in only match.

1 match for Hants 1905.

Was a Regular Army officer.

S.G. Shepherd

G.H.T. Simpson-Hayward

A. Shutt

SHORTING, Wilfred Lionel – RHB
b. Tenbury Wells, W, 12 March 1904; d. Hastings, Sussex, 10 October 1982. Educated at King's School, Worcester.

Debut 1922 v Hants, Southampton. 9 matches for W (amateur) 1922–26. Highest score: W 27 v Notts., Trent Bridge 1926.

SHUTT, Albert – RHB RM
b. Stockton-on-Tees, Co. Durham, 21 September 1952. Educated at Stockton Grammar School.

Debut 1972 v Glam., Worcester. 2 matches for W 1972. Did not bat. Best bowling: 1–36 on debut.

Minor Counties for Durham 1977. Birmingham League cricket for Stourbridge and Old Hill. Played Thornaby and Stockton in North East.

SIMPSON-HAYWARD, George Hayward Thomas – RHB RAB of slow underarm lobs
b. Stoneleigh, War., 7 June 1875; d. Icomb, Glos., 2 October 1936. Educated at Malvern and Clare College, Cambridge U.

Debut 1899 v Sussex, Hove. 156 matches for W 1899–1914 (amateur). Highest score: W 130 v Oxford U, Oxford 1911. Best bowling: W 7–54 v Middx., Lord's 1909.

3 matches for Cambridge U 1895–97 (no Blue). 5 tests for England v S. Africa 1909/10; 15 test runs (15.00); 23 test wickets (18.26). Best test

bowling; 6–43 v South Africa, Jo'burg (test debut) 1909/10. 5548 first-class runs (18.61); 500 wickets (21.41).

SINGLETON, Alexander Parkinson ('Sandy') – RHB SLA
b. Repton, Derby., 5 August 1914. Educated at Shrewsbury and Brasenose College, Oxford U. Debut 1934 v Som., Frome. 58 matches for W 1934–46. Capped; captain 1946 (amateur). Highest score: W 164 v War., Edgbaston 1946. Best bowling: W 4–30 v Northants, Worcester 1936. 1615 runs (37.55) in 1946.

    42 matches Oxford U 1934–37 (Blue each season; capt. 1937). Played Rhodesia 1946/47–1949/50. Best first-class bowling: 6–44 Oxford U v Leveson-Gower's XI, Reigate 1934. 4700 first-class runs (27.65); 240 wickets (30.49).

    Brother G.M. Singleton (W).

SINGLETON, George Michael – RHB SLA
b. Repton, Derby., 12 May 1913. Educated at Uppingham and Pembroke College, Cambridge U.

    Debut 1946 v Combined Services, Worcester. 2 matches for W (amateur) 1946. Highest score: W 23 v Combined Services, Worcester on debut. Best bowling: W 1–1 v Som., Weston-super-Mare 1946.

    Brother A.P. Singleton (W).

A.P. Singleton

G.M. Singleton

D.J. Smith

D.N.F. Slade

SLADE, Douglas Norman Frank – RHB SLA
b. Feckenham, 24 August 1940.

Debut 1958 v Som., Taunton. 266 matches for W (professional) 1958–71. Cap 1960; benefit 1971. Highest score: W 125 v Leics., Leicester 1969. Best bowling: W 7–47 v Middx., Lord's 1960. Took 97 wickets (19.83) in 1960.

Played Shrops. in Minor Counties Championship 1973–78. Birmingham League cricket for West Bromwich Dartmouth and Worcester City.

SMITH, Douglas James – RHB SRA
b. Batley, Yorks., 29 May 1873; d. Grahamstown, S. Africa, 16 August 1949.

Debut 1901 v Lancs., Old Trafford. 9 matches for W 1901–04 (professional). Highest score: W 29 v Lancs., Old Trafford 1902.

21 matches Som. 1896–98. Highest first-class score 62, Som. v Middx., Lord's. Played Glam. 1905–07 in Minor County matches.

Brother William Smith (Som.); father John Smith (Yorks; also W groundsman).

SMITH, David Mark – LHB RM
b. Balham, London, 9 January 1956. Educated at Battersea Grammar School.

Debut 1984 v Sussex, Worcester. 56 matches for W 1984–86. Cap 1984. Highest score: W 189* v Kent, Worcester 1984. Best bowling: W 2–35 v Surrey, the Oval 1986.

168 matches Surrey 1973–83 and 1987–88. Cap 1980. 19 matches for Sussex 1989. 1000 runs (3) for W – 1113 (46.37) 1985 best. 2 tests for England v W. Indies 1985/86. 80 runs (20.00). Highest score 47 at Port-of-Spain.

Fiery temper has caused difficulty with all his three counties: back trouble has lately interfered with career.

SMITH, Ernest Somers – RHB
b. Sheffield, Yorks., 1895; d. Bradford, Yorks., 1950.

Debut 1921 v Essex, Leyton. 2 matches for W 1921 (amateur). Highest score W 22 v Essex, Leyton 1921 on debut.

SMITH, James Crosbie – LHB
b. Ledbury, Herefordshire, 26 September 1894; d. Ledbury, 19 February 1980.

Debut 1923 v Essex, Leyton. 16 matches for W 1923–25 as professional. Highest score: W 70 v Notts., Stourbridge 1923.

SMITH, Lawrence Kilner – RHB
b. Mirfield, Yorks., 6 January 1964. Educated at Stancliffe Hall, Derby. and St Andrew's College, Welkom, S. Africa and King Edward's School, Jo'burg.

Debut 1985 v Cambridge U, Cambridge. 4 matches for W 1985–87.

D.M. Smith

J.C. Smith

L.K. Smith

Highest score: W 28 v Cambridge U, Cambridge 1985 (on debut). Best bowling: W 1–20 v War., Worcester 1987.

Birmingham League cricket for Walsall. Played for Durban Collegians in S. Africa.

Father D.H.K. Smith (Derby. and Orange Free State).

SOLLY, Edward Walter – LHB LFM
b. Eastry, Kent, 7 May 1882; d. Cefn Mably, Glam., 12 February 1966.

Debut 1903 v Cambridge U, Cambridge. 8 matches for W (professional) 1903–07. Highest score: W 43 v Oxford U, Worcester 1904. Best bowling: W 3–25 v Glos., Worcester 1905.

SOMERS, Lord (Arthur Herbert Tennyson Somers-Cocks) – RHB
b. Isle of Wight, 20 March 1887; d. Eastnor, Hants, 14 July 1944. Educated at Charterhouse.

Debut 1923 v Glos., Bristol. 16 matches for W 1923–35. Highest score W 52 v Essex, Leyton 1925. 1 first-class match MCC 1906.

SOUTHALL, Harry – RHB
b. Stourbridge area.

Debut 1907 v Lancs., Stourbridge. 1 match for W 1907. 11 in only innings.

Played Stourbridge in Birmingham League.

SPENCER, Alan Horace – RHB OB
b. Lee Green, Kent, 4 July 1936.

Debut 1957 v Oxford U, Oxford. 27 matches for W (professional) 1957–61. Highest score: W 85 v Northants, Dudley 1960. Birmingham League cricket for Dudley.

SPENCER, Harry Norman Ernest – RHB RM
b. Shipston-on-Stour, War., 1 October 1901; d. Hammersmith, London, 13 August 1954.

Debut 1927 v New Zealand, Worcester. 1 match for W 1927 (amateur). Highest score: W 26 v New Zealand, Worcester 1927. Best bowling: 1–34, same match.

1 match for War. 1930, for which team took wicket with first ball (v W!). Club cricket for Stratford-upon-Avon and Coventry and North War.

SPILSBURY, John William Edward – RHB RFM
b. Worcester, 27 October 1933.

Debut 1952 v Combined Services, Worcester. 1 match for W 1952 (amateur). Highest score: 16 in only match.

Grandfather G.F. Wheldon (W).

STANDEN, James Alfred – RHB LB/RM
b. Edmonton, London, 30 May 1935.

Debut 1959 v Oxford U, Worcester. 133 matches for W 1959–70. Cap 1962. Highest score: W 92* v Oxford U, Oxford 1970. Best bowling: W 7–30 v Oxford U, Halesowen 1964.

Minor Counties cricket for Herts. 1956–57.

Top class soccer goalkeeper for Arsenal, Luton, West Ham, Portsmouth, Millwall, and Detroit Cougars.

J.A. Standen

J. Stanning

STANNING, John – RHB
b. London, 24 June 1919. Educated at Winchester and Christ Church College, Oxford U.

Debut 1939 v Som., Kidderminster. 9 matches for W 1939–46 (amateur). Highest score: W 56* v Northants, Rushden 1939.

Qualified by living at Upton-on-Severn. Father J. Stanning (Lancs.).

STEPHENSON, John William Arthur – RHB RFM
b. Hong Kong, 1 August 1907; d. Pulborough, Sussex, 20 May 1982. Educated at Claysmore School, RMC Sandhurst.

Debut 1947 v Leics., Kidderminster. 1 match for W (amateur) 1947. Highest score W 12 in match above. Took 1 wicket in only match.

61 matches for Essex 1934–39; capped, and joint-captain 1939. First-class cricket for the Army, 1931–38, and in India for European teams in tournaments at Madras and Bombay. Highest first-class score: 135, Europeans v Parsees, Bombay 1928/29. Best first-class bowling: 9–46, Gentlemen v Players, Lord's 1936. Played in one 'Victory Test' against Australia in 1945. Minor Counties cricket for Bucks 1931–32. Birmingham League cricket for Kidderminster.

Regular Army officer (Lt-Colonel).

STEVENS, Bertie Grosvenor – RHB WK
b. Thingoe, Suffolk, 9 April 1886; d. Wednesbury, Staffs., March 1943. Educated at Cheltenham and Worcester Royal Grammar School.

Debut 1905 v Lancs., Worcester. 18 matches for W 1905–14 (amateur). Highest score: W 41 v Leics., Coalville 1914.

1 match for H.K. Foster's XI 1919 *against* W. Birmingham League cricket for Dudley.

STEWART, David Ernest Robertson – RHB OB
b. Bombay, India, 22 May 1948. Educated at Robert Gordon's College and Cathedral High School, Bombay.

Debut 1970 v Som., Worcester. 23 matches for W 1970–73. Highest score: W 69 v New Zealand, Worcester 1973.

9 matches for Scotland 1969–79. 854 first-class runs (17.79). Birmingham League cricket for Stourbridge and Old Hill. Scottish Club cricket for Ferguslie, Dunbartonshire and Selkirk.

STIMPSON, Peter John – RHB RM
b. Aberfan, S. Wales, 25 May 1947. Educated at Cathay's High School, Cardiff.

Debut 1971 v Oxford U, Oxford. 30 matches for W 1971–72. Highest score: W 103 v Glam., Worcester 1971. Twice shared century opening stands in each innings with R.G.A. Headley in 1971 – the first four times they opened together.

Birmingham League cricket for West Bromwich Dartmouth.

B.G. Stevens

P.J. Stimpson

S.W. Styler

T. Straw

STRAW, Thomas – RHB WK
b. Hucknall Torkard, Notts., 1 September 1870; d. Hucknall Torkard, 5 September 1959.

Debut 1899 v Yorks., Worcester. 61 matches for W 1899–1907 (professional). Highest score: W 32 v Glos., Gloucester 1900 (added 56 for 10th wicket with A. Bird – then a county record).

Unique in being dismissed twice 'obstructed the field' – both times against War., in 1899 and 1901.

STRINGER, Thomas – LB
b. in Yorks. about 1874; dead.

Debut 1909 v Lancs., Stourbridge. 1 match for W (professional) 1909. Scored 0 and 0* and took 1 wicket in only match.

Birmingham League cricket for Dudley.

STYLER, Sidney William – RHB WK
b. Cotteridge, Birmingham, 20 August 1908; d. Worcester, 27 January 1980.

Debut 1929 v Glos., Worcester. 18 matches for W 1929–31 (professional). Highest score: 24 v Northants, Northampton 1929.

SUCKLING, Ernest – LHB SLA
b. Balsall Heath, Birmingham, 27 March 1890; d. Blackpool, 24 February 1962.

Debut 1923 v Lancs., Worcester. 3 matches for W 1923–24 (professional). Highest score: W 58 v Kent, Dudley 1923. Best bowling W 4–71 v Lancs., Worcester 1923 (debut).

2 matches for War. 1919.

SUMMERS, Douglas Walter Levi – RHB SLA
b. Smethwick, Staffs., 12 October 1911.
Debut 1930 v War., Dudley. 1 match for W (professional) 1930. 4 runs in only innings. 0 wickets.
Father F.T. Summers (W).

SUMMERS, Francis Theodore – RHB WK
b. Alcester, War., 25 January 1887; d. Inkberrow, 27 October 1967.
Debut 1921 v Derby., Chesterfield. 57 matches for W (professional) 1921–28. Highest score: W 36 v Derby., Kidderminster 1928.
Son D.W.L. Summers (W). Played Astwood Bank CC.

SUTOR, John Allan – RHB RM
b. Knighton-on-Teme, Tenbury, 1 July 1909; d. in Australia, December 1966. Educated at Uppingham.
Debut 1928 v Hants, Worcester. 1 match for W (amateur) 1928. Scored 2 and 1 in only match.

SWALWELL, Reginald Sawdon – LHB; occ. bowler.
b. York, 25 June 1873; d. Sunningdale, Berks., 20 September 1930.
Debut 1907 v Yorks., Worcester. 18 matches for W 1907–20 (amateur). Highest score: W 57 v Oxford U, Oxford 1908.
Various first-class games for MCC 1914–25. Highest first-class score 72 MCC v Cambridge U, Lord's 1921. Minor Counties for Dorset 1903–05.

D.W.L. Summers

F.T. Summers

T

TARBOX, Charles Victor – RHB RM
b. Hemel Hempstead, Herts., 2 July 1891; d. Peacehaven, Sussex, 16 June 1978.

Debut 1921 v Essex, Leyton. 226 matches for W 1921–29 (professional). Highest score: W 109 v Notts, Trent Bridge 1927. Best bowling: W 7–55 v Som., Worcester 1921. Added 141 for 9th wicket with W.V. Fox v War., Edgbaston 1929 – second highest 9th wicket stand for County.

Played for Herts. in Minor Counties Championship 1931–33.

TASKER, Alfred George Ernest – RHB WK
b. Southwark, London, 16 June 1934. Educated at William Ellis Grammar School, London.

Debut 1956 v Cambridge U, Cambridge. 1 match for W 1956 (professional). Did not bat or bowl.

On Lord's staff 1955–56. Club cricket in London area for Wembley and Turnham Green.

A.G.E. Tasker

C.V. Tarbox

W.R.K. Thomas

W.H. Taylor

TAYLOR, Robert Joseph – RHB RM
b. Liverpool, 1 November 1873; death unknown.
  Debut 1900 v London County, Crystal Palace. 1 match for W
(professional) 1900. Scored 1 and 0, took 0 wickets.
  2 matches for Lancs. 1898.
  On Old Trafford ground staff until 1900.

TAYLOR, William Herbert – RHB RMF
b. Sale, Ches., 23 June 1885; d. Birlingham, Worcs., 27 May 1959.
  Debut 1909 v Kent, Tonbridge. 109 matches for W 1909–25 (amateur);
captain 1914–19; 1922. Highest score: W 59* v Essex, Worcester 1914.
Best bowling: W 7–64 v Glam., Kidderminster 1921.

THOMAS, William Richard Keay – RHB RM
b. Redditch, 22 July 1960. Educated at Dean Close School, Cheltenham.
  Debut 1981 v Sri Lanka, Worcester. Scored 44 and 13* in only match.

THORNYCROFT, Guy Mytton – RHB
b. Ulverston, Lancs., 1 April 1917. Educated at Shrewsbury.
Debut 1947 v Combined Services, Hereford. 1 match for W 1947 (amateur). Scored 3 and 0 in only match.
Played for Services v 'Indian XI', Calcutta 1945.

THORP, Philip – RHB
b. Kidderminster, 6 May 1911.
Debut 1935 v Surrey, Worcester. 2 matches for W 1935 (amateur). Highest score: W 11 v Surrey, Worcester on debut.
Birmingham League cricket for Kidderminster.

THURSFIELD, John Hunt – RHB
b. Alvechurch, 16 June 1892; d. Shenstone, Staffs., 26 April 1951. Educated at Shrewsbury.
Debut 1922 v War., Edgbaston. 3 matches for W (amateur) 1922–25. Highest score for W 35 v Warwicks., Edgbaston 1922 on debut.
Club cricket for Middlesbrough and Guisborough.

TINKLER, Edgar – RHB RM
b. Burnley, Lancs., 11 March 1921. Educated at Worcester Royal Grammar School.
Debut 1953 v Northants, Worcester (amateur). 1 match for W 1953 (amateur). Highest score: W 7 v Northants, Worcester 1953 (in only match).

P. Thorp

G.M. Thornycroft

J.H. Thursfield

F.M. Tomkinson

2 first-class matches for MCC 1960–61. Captained Worcester Second XI on occasion. Birmingham League cricket for Dudley; also played Worcester City.

TIPPER, Benjamin Claude Cecil – RHB
b. Birmingham, 7 July 1896; d. Norton Lindsey, War., 11 July 1970. Educated at King Edwards, Birmingham.
Debut 1919 v Glos., Worcester. 5 matches for W (amateur) 1919. Highest score: W 43 v War., Worcester 1919. Best bowling: W 2–0 v Glos., Cheltenham 1919.

TOLLEY, Christopher Mark – RHB LM
b. Kidderminster, 30 December 1967. Educated at King Edward VI School, Stourbridge.
Debut 1989 v Surrey, Worcester. Highest score: W 37 v Kent, Worcester 1989.
Birmingham League cricket for Stourbridge.

TOMKINSON, Francis Martin – RHB
b. Kidderminster, 21 October 1883; d. Cleobury Mortimer, Shrops., 24 November 1963. Educated at Eton.
Debut 1902 v Hants, Worcester. 1 match for W (amateur) 1902. Scored 0 in only innings.
Birmingham League cricket for Kidderminster. Brother Sir G.S. Tomkinson (W).

TOMKINSON, Sir Geoffrey Stewart – RHB
b. Kidderminster, 7 November 1881; d. Kidderminster, 8 February 1963. Educated at Winchester and King's College, Cambridge U.

Debut 1903 v Cambridge U, Cambridge. 2 matches for W (amateur) 1903–26 (an interval of 23 years). Highest score: W 10 v Derby., Kidderminster 1926. W CCC President 1956–58.

Birmingham League cricket for Kidderminster. Played Rugby Union for Kidderminster.

Work in carpet trade prevented more frequent appearances. Brother F.M. Tomkinson (W).

TOPPIN, Charles Graham – RHB OB
b. Upton-on-Severn, 17 April 1906; d. Leamington Spa, War., 20 May 1972. Educated at Malvern.

Debut 1927 v Lancs., Nelson. 4 matches for W 1927–28 (amateur). Highest score: W 10 v Lancs., Worcester 1928.

C. Toppin (Cambridge U 1885–87) father; J.F.T. Toppin (W) brother; S.H., A.P. and S.E. Day (all Kent) were his uncles.

TOPPIN, John Fallowfield Townsend – RHB RMF
b. Malvern, W, 25 February 1900; d. Ascot, Berks., 22 November 1965. Educated at Winchester.

Debut 1920 v Lancs., Old Trafford. 1 match for W (amateur) 1920. Scored 2 and 6, and took 0 wickets in only match.

Father C. Toppin (Cambridge U); brother C.G. Toppin (W); uncles A.P., S.E. and S.H. Day (all Kent).

Sir G.S. Tomkinson

C.G. Toppin

J.F.T. Toppin

G.M. Turner

TURNER, Glenn Maitland – RHB OB
b. Dunedin, New Zealand, 26 May 1947. Educated at Otago High School.

Debut 1967 v Pakistan, Worcester. 284 matches for W 1967–82. Cap 1968; benefit (£21,103) 1978; captain 1981. Highest score: W 311* v War., Worcester 1982. Best bowling: W 3–18 v Pakistan, Worcester 1967 (on debut). 1000 runs (14) – 2379 (61.00) 1970 best. Also scored 2101 runs (55.28) in 1981. In addition to highest score also scored: 239* v Oxford U, Oxford 1982; 228* v Glos., Worcester 1980; 214* v Oxford U, Worcester 1975; 202* v Cambridge U, Cambridge 1974; 202* v War., Edgbaston 1978. Carried bat through innings twice – 88*/202 v Som., Worcester 1972; 141*/169 v Glam., Swansea 1977 (this latter, 83.4% of a completed innings is a world record). Scored hundred in each innings three times – 122 and 128* v War., Edgbaston 1972; 161 and 101 v Northants, Stourbridge 1981; 147* and 139 v War., Worcester 1981. Century before lunch, a record for county of 8 times. 72 centuries for W – county record. 10 centuries in 1970 – county record.

Played domestic cricket in New Zealand 1964/65 to 1982/83; for Otago and Northern Districts. 41 tests for New Zealand 1968/69–82/83 (captain on 10 occasions). 2991 test runs (44.64). Highest test score: 259 v W. Indies, Georgetown 1971/72. 34346 first-class runs (49.71); 103 centuries – in 1982 became 19th player to score 100 centuries with his 311* v War. Remains the only New Zealander to perform this feat. Added 387 for 1st wicket with T.W. Jarvis, New Zealand v W. Indies, Georgetown 1971/72 – New Zealand test record for any wicket. Became 7th batsman to score 1000 runs before the end of May in 1973. In 1979 became first batsman to score first-class hundreds against every county. Birmingham League cricket for Stourbridge.

TURNER, James William Cecil – RHB occ. bowler.

b. Bromley, Kent, 2 October 1886; d. Cambridge, 29 November 1968.

Debut 1911 v Glos., Cheltenham. 48 matches for W 1911–21 (amateur). Highest score: W 106 v Northants, Northampton 1921.

Was a medical practitioner.

TURNER, Richard Ernest – RHB RM

b. Mitcham, Surrey, 4 May 1888; d. Hastings, Sussex, 16 March 1967.

Debut 1909 v Kent, Stourbridge. 52 matches for W (professional) 1909–22. Highest score: W 66 v War., Worcester 1911. Best bowling: W 3–7 v Kent, Maidstone 1911.

Played and coached Green Point CC, S. Africa after retirement from W.

J.W.C. Turner

VORSTER, Louis Phillipus – LHB ROB
b. Potchefstroom, S. Africa 2 November 1966. Educated Potchefstroom High School and Rand Afrikaans U.

Debut 1988 v W. Indies, Worcester. 1 match for W 1988. Highest score W 16* in only innings. Did not bowl in only match.

Has played for Transvaal since 1985/86. Highest first-class score: 174 Transvaal v W. Province, Cape Town 1987/88. 1497 first-class runs (33.26). Birmingham League cricket for Old Hill and Kidderminster; also played for Halesowen.

L.P. Vorster

WAKEFIELD, Percy Harold – RHB RM
b. Pill, Som., 3 September 1888; d. Worcester, 20 December 1973.
Educated at Taunton.
Debut 1922 v Hants, Worcester 1922. 1 match for W (amateur) 1922.
Scored 0 and 8 in only match.

WAKELIN, Edwin – RHB Slow bowler
b. Cowley St John, Oxford, 18 October 1880; d. St Giles, Headington,
Oxford, 13 August 1925.
Debut 1910 v Essex, Bournville. 1 match for W (professional) 1910.
Scored 6 in only innings.
Played Oxford. in Minor Counties Championship 1922–24.

WALFORD, John Erskine Scott – RHB RFM
b. Hanbury, 14 August 1899; d. in hospital, Ravenscourt Park, London,
22 August 1961. Educated at Malvern.
Debut 1923 v Sussex, Hastings. 6 matches for W 1923–30 (amateur).
Highest score: W 31 v Northants, Northampton.
Played first-class cricket for the Army 1930–32. Best first-class bowling
6–27, Army v MCC, Lord's 1930. 29 first-class wickets (16.14).
Regular Army officer.

WALLACE, Charles William – RHB
b. Sunderland, Co. Durham, 24 November 1884; d. Awbridge, Hants, 5
September 1946. Educated at Winchester.
Debut 1921 v Glos., Stourbridge 1921. 4 matches for W 1921–22
(amateur). Highest score: 39* v Hants, Worcester 1922.
Major in Regular Army.

WALTERS, Cyril Frederick – RHB
b. Bedlinog, Glam., 28 August 1905.
Debut 1928 v West Indies, Worcester (after several Championship
appearances for Glam. earlier the same season). 137 matches for W

C.F. Walters

F.B. Warne

(amateur) 1928–35 (capped). Captain 1931–35. Highest score: W 226 v Kent, Gravesend 1933. Best bowling: W 2–22 v Northants, Worcester 1933. 1000 runs (5) – 2292 (53.30) 1933 best. 9 centuries in 1933 – County record until beaten by G.M. Turner in 1970.

75 matches for Glam. 1923–28. 11 tests for England 1933–34. 784 test runs (52.26). Highest test score: 102 v India, Madras 1933/34. Captain v Australia, Trent Bridge 1934, when R.E.S. Wyatt was unavailable. 12145 first-class runs (30.74) with 21 centuries.

WARNE, Frank Belmont – LHB ROB
b. North Carlton, Melbourne, Victoria, 3 October 1906.

Debut 1934 v Cambridge U, Worcester. 95 matches for W 1934–38 (professional – capped). Highest score: W 115 v Lancs., Old Trafford 1936. Best bowling: W 6–51 v Northants, Northampton 1935. 1000 runs (20.40) in 1935.

Played for Victoria 1926/27 until 1928/29; Europeans, in India 1934/35, until 1937/38 and Transvaal 1941/42. Also toured India with a private Australian team 1935/36. Scored 108 for 'The Rest of South Africa' against 'An Airforce XI' at Johannesburg, December 1942, his last appearance in first-class cricket. 3275 first-class runs (21.40); 138 wickets (34.78).

Father, T.S. Warne, played for Victoria.

WARNER, Allan Esmond – RHB RFM
b. Birmingham, 12 May 1957. Educated at Tabernacle School, St Kitts.

Debut 1982 v Derby., Worcester. 28 matches for W 1982–84. Highest score: W 67 v War., Edgbaston 1982. Best bowling: W 5–27 v Glam., Worcester 1984.

87 matches for Derby. 1985–date (cap 1987). Highest first-class score: 91 Derby. v Leics., Chesterfield 1986. 2384 first-class runs (18.33); 230 wickets (31.12). Birmingham League cricket for Mitchells & Butlers.

WATKINS, Stephen George – RHB
b. Hereford, 23 March 1959. Educated at Lady Hankin's School, Kington.

Debut 1983 v Oxford U, Oxford. 1 match for W 1983; scored 77 and 28 in only match.

Birmingham League cricket for Worcester City; also played Hereford Town Club.

WATSON, Gregory George – RHB RFM
b. Mudgee, New South Wales, Australia, 29 January 1955. Educated at

S.G. Watkins

A.E. Warner

G.G. Watson

A.J. Webster

Mudgee High School, U of New South Wales.
   Debut 1978 v Pakistan, Worcester 1978. 30 matches for W 1978–79.
Highest score: W 38 v Som., Taunton 1978. Best bowling: W 6–45 v
Sussex, Eastbourne 1978.
   Played Australian domestic cricket for New South Wales (14) 1977–79
and Western Australia (1) 1979/80. 552 first-class runs (12.83); 102
wickets (37.56). Birmingham League cricket for Smethwick and
Stourbridge.

WEBSTER, Andrew John – LHB RMF
b. Rolleston-on-Dove, Staffs., 5 March 1959. Educated at Forest of
Needwood High School.
   Debut 1981 v Kent, Canterbury. 9 matches for W 1981–82. Highest
score: W 25 v War., Edgbaston 1982. Best bowling: W 5–87 v Hants,
Southampton 1982.
   Minor Counties cricket for Staffs. since 1980. Birmingham League
cricket for Old Hill; also plays for Burton-on-Trent CC.

WELLS, Thomas Umphrey – LHB; useful bowler
b. Panmure, New Zealand, 6 February 1927. Educated at King's College, Auckland; Auckland U; King's College, Cambridge U.
Debut 1950 v Som., Worcester. 1 match for W (amateur) 1950; Scored 0 and 9 in only match.
20 matches for Cambridge U, 1950 and 1951: Blue 1950. Highest first-class score: 77*, Cambridge U v Leics., Cambridge 1950. Best first-class bowling 2–25, Cambridge U v Hants, Cambridge 1950.
Won Rugby Union Blue for Cambridge and had England trial.

WESTON, Martin John – RHB RM
b. Worcester, 8 April 1959. Educated at Samuel Southall Secondary School.
Debut 1979 v Sri Lanka, Worcester. 143 matches for W 1979–date. Highest score: W 145* v Northants, Worcester 1984. Best bowling: W 4–24 v War., Edgbaston 1988. 1061 runs (27.92) in 1984.
Birmingham League cricket for Old Hill and Worcester City.

WHELDON, George Frederick – RHB WK
b. Langley Green, 1 November 1869; d. Worcester, 13 January 1924.
Debut 1899 v Yorks., Worcester. 138 matches for W 1899–1906 (professional). Highest score: W 112 v Som., Worcester 1903.
Birmingham League cricket for Dudley.

T.U. Wells

M.J. Weston

G.F. Wheldon

P.J. Whitcombe

Top-class Association footballer for Aston Villa, West Bromwich Albion, Coventry, Queens Park Rangers, Portsmouth and England.
Grandson J.W.E. Spilsbury played for W.

WHITCOMBE, Philip John – RHB WK
b. Worcester, 11 November 1928. Educated at Worcester Royal Grammar School and Hertford College, Oxford U.
Debut 1949 v Cambridge U, Worcester. 8 matches for W (amateur) 1949–52. Highest score: W 89* v Hants, Bournemouth, 1952.
26 matches Oxford U 1950–52 (Blue 1951–52). Highest first-class score: 104, Oxford U v Hants, Basingstoke 1951. Played club cricket for Brentwood, where he taught.

White, M.E.

A.F.T. White

WHITE, Allan Frederick Tinsdale – RHB
b. Coventry, War., 5 September 1915. Educated at Uppingham and Pembroke College, Cambridge U.
Debut 1939 v Surrey, The Oval. 110 matches for W (amateur) 1939–49 (cap 1946). Captain 1947–48; joint captain with R.E.S. Wyatt 1949. Highest score: W 95 v Combined Services, Worcester 1946.
Played 22 matches for Cambridge U 1936–37 (Blue 1936). 9 matches for War. 1936–37. Birmingham League cricket for Moseley.

WHITE, Montague Eric – RHB RF
b. London, 21 January 1908; d. Birkenhead, Wirral, Ches., 21 June 1970. Educated at Worcester Royal Grammar School.
Debut 1931 v Northants, Worcester. 34 matches for W 1931–34 (professional). Highest score: W 37 v Essex, Worcester 1931. Best bowling: W 5–34 v Northants, Worcester 1931 (on debut).

WHITEHEAD, John Parkin – RHB RFM
b. Saddleworth, Yorks., 3 September 1925. Educated at Oldham Grammar School and London U.
Debut 1953 v Australians, Worcester. 33 matches for W 1953–55 (professional). Highest score: W 71 v Derby., Worcester 1954. Best bowling: W 5–89 v Australians. Worcester 1953 (on debut).
37 matches Yorks., 1947–51; also played for Combined Services 1947. Best first-class bowling: 5–10, Combined Services v W., Hereford 1947.

1246 first-class runs (19.17); 147 wickets (29.23). Played for various clubs in North of England including Pudsey St Laurence in Bradford League; in 1953 was suspended by Bradford League for five years for breaking contract with them to sign for W.

Has B.Sc degree from London University.

WHITING, Norman Harry – RHB OB

b. Wollaston, Stourbridge, 2 October 1920. Educated at Wollaston School.

Debut 1947 v Northants, Wellingborough. 59 matches for W 1947–52 (professional) cap 1950). Highest score: W 118 v Essex, Romford 1950. Best bowling: W 2–27 v Yorks., Scarborough 1951.

Birmingham League cricket for Stourbridge.

On W CCC Committee for many years; spends much time at the ground. Former skipper of W 2nd XI.

WILCOCK, Howard Gordon – RHB WK

b. New Malden, Surrey, 26 February 1950. Educated at Giggleswick School, Settle, Yorks.

Debut 1971 v Oxford U, Oxford 1971. 99 matches for W 1971–78. Highest score: W 74 v Yorks., Worcester 1977. 6 dismissals (all ct) in

N.H. Whiting

J.P. Whitehead

H.G. Wilcock

A.J. Wilkes

innings v Hants, Portsmouth 1974 – equalling W record for County Championship.

Birmingham League cricket for Stourbridge and Duport.

WILKES, Alexander John – RHB

b. Kidderminster, 4 November 1900; d. Kidderminster, 12 July 1937.

Debut 1925 v Northants, Northampton. 11 matches for W (amateur) 1925–27. Highest score: W 25 v Kent, Folkestone 1927.

Birmingham League cricket for Kidderminster.

Father W.H.W. Wilkes (W).

WILKES, William Harry Walters – RHB

b. Birmingham, 1866; d. Birmingham, 18 February 1940.

Debut 1899 v Yorks., Sheffield. 14 matches for W (amateur) 1899–1902. Highest score: W 109 v Yorks., Dewsbury 1901.

Birmingham League cricket for Kidderminster.

Son A.J. Wilkes (W).

WILKINSON, John William – RHB; bowler
b. Dudley, 20 April 1892; d. Edgbaston cricket ground, 3 August 1967.
  Debut 1927 v Lancs., Dudley. 1 match for W (amateur) 1927. Scored 4* and 0* in only match; 1 wicket.
  Played for Devon in Minor Counties Championship 1925.
  Collapsed and died while acting as War. scorer, v Scotland at Edgbaston.

WILKINSON, Keith William – LHB LM
b. Fenton, Stoke-on-Trent, 15 January 1950.
  Debut 1969 v Som., Weston-super-Mare. 49 matches for W 1969–75.

J.W. Wilkinson

W.H.W. Wilkes

K.W. Wilkinson

R.H. Williams

Highest score: W 141 v Oxford U, Oxford 1974. Best bowling: W 5–60 v Sussex, Worcester 1971.
 Birmingham League cricket for Stourbridge and Old Hill.

WILLIAMS, H. – B SLA
Debut 1927 v Sussex, Hove 1927. 4 matches for W (professional) 1927.
Highest score: W 4 v Glos., Worcester 1927. Best bowling: W 1–13 v Glam., Pontypridd 1927.

WILLIAMS, Richard Harry – LHB
b. Brockmoor, Staffs., 23 April 1901; d. Stourbridge, 19 December 1982.
 Debut 1923 v Derby., Dudley. 37 matches for W 1923–32 (amateur).
Highest score: W 76* v Yorks., Worcester 1928.
 Birmingham League cricket for Stourbridge.

WILSON, George Alfred – RHB RF
b. Amersham, Bucks., 5 April 1877; d. Abbotts Langley, Herts., 3 March 1962.

Debut 1899 v Yorks., Worcester. 154 matches for W 1899–1906 (professional). Highest score: W 78 v London County, Worcester 1900. (These runs were scored in only 50 minutes; 97 runs added for 10th wicket with A. Bird, a W 10th-wicket record until 1906, when beaten by stand of 119 between Wilson and W.B. Burns v Som., Worcester. These remain the two best W 10th-wicket stands.) Best bowling: W 9–75 v Oxford U, Oxford 1905. Also took 15–142 in match (8–30, 7–112) v Som., Taunton 1905. 100 wickets (3) – 119 (22.36) 1901 best. Three hat tricks: v London County, Worcester 1900; v Surrey, Worcester 1901; v Australians, Worcester 1905.

Minor Counties Championship for Bucks. 1907–08; Staffs, 1912–14. Birmingham League cricket for Kidderminster.

Son G.C. Wilson (W).

WILSON, George Clifford – RHB RF
b. Kidderminster, 27 July 1902; d. Elswich, Newcastle upon Tyne, 18 May 1957.

Debut 1924 v War., Edgbaston. 70 matches for W 1924–26 (professional). Highest score: W 40 v Essex, Worcester 1926. Best bowling: W 8–81 v Som., Weston-super-Mare 1926.

Played Minor Counties cricket for Northumb. 1935–47.

Father G.A. Wilson (W).

G.A. Wilson

G.C. Wilson

G.T.O. Wilson

WILSON, Grenville Thomas Owen – LHB LFM
b. Elmsley Lovett, 9 April 1932. Educated at Hartlebury Grammar School.

Debut 1951 v Northants, Northampton. 13 matches for W (professional) 1951–53. Highest score: W 4* v Surrey, Kidderminster 1952. Best bowling: W 3–42 v Middx., Lord's 1952.

Birmingham League cricket for Kidderminster and Old Hill.

WILSON, Harry – LHB SLA
b. Yorks., 1873; d. Kidderminster, 13 August 1906 (of a brain haemorrhage after sunstroke).

Debut 1901 v South Africa, Worcester. 6 matches for W (professional) 1901-06. Highest score: W 21 v Kent, Worcester 1906. Best bowling: W 6–86 v Surrey, The Oval 1903.

Birmingham League cricket for Kidderminster.

WINNINGTON, John Francis Sartorius – RHB
b. Martley, 17 September 1876; d. in action, Ramle, Palestine, 22 September 1918.

Debut 1908 v Oxford U, Oxford (amateur). 1 match for W; 20 and 0 in only match.

Played for W Gentlemen.

In regular army – reached rank of Lt.-Colonel.

WINWOOD, Thomas Lawson – RHB
b. Dudley, 7 February 1910.
   Debut 1930 v Derby., Kidderminster. 18 matches for W 1930–34 (amateur). Highest score W: 104 v Hants, Worcester 1930.
   Birmingham League cricket for Kidderminster.

WRIGHT, Leslie – RHB RM
b. in County Durham, 20 January 1903; d. London, 6 January 1956.
   Debut 1925 v Oxford U, Oxford. 193 matches for W 1925–33 (professional). Highest score: W 134 v Northants, Northampton 1930. Best bowling: W 3–6 v Hants, Dudley 1932. 1000 runs (2) – 1402 runs (24.17) 1928 best.
   Birmingham League cricket for Stourbridge.
   In later life ran a remand home in Mitcham, Surrey.

WYATT, Robert Elliott Storey – RHB RMF
b. Milford, Surrey, 2 May 1901. Educated at King Henry VIII School, Coventry.
   Debut 1946 v War., Dudley. 86 matches for W 1946–51 (amateur – cap 1946). Joint-captain 1949; captain 1950–51. Highest score: W 166* v Sussex, Worcester 1947. Also scored 166 v Surrey, Worcester 1948. Best bowling: W 5–43 v Essex, Worcester 1948.

L. Wright

R.E.S. Wyatt

A. Wyers

Played 404 matches for War. 1923–39; captain 1930–37. 40 test matches for England 1927–37, captain on 16 occasions. Test record: 1839 runs (31.70); 2 centuries; 18 wickets (35.66). Highest test score: 149 v South Africa, Trent Bridge 1935; Best test bowling 3–4 v South Africa, Durban 1927/28. Highest first-class score: 232, War. v Derby., Edgbaston 1937. Best first-class bowling: 7–34 War. v Middx., Lord's 1926. Scored 1000 runs in a season (all first-class matches) 17 times – best was 2630 (53.67) in 1929. Full first-class record: 39405 runs (40.04); 85 centuries; 901 wickets (32.84).

Played last first-class match for Free Foresters in 1957 aged 56. Birmingham League cricket for Moseley; also played Meriden CC. Test selector 1949–53 (Chairman 1950).

Autobiography: *Three Straight Sticks* (1961).

WYERS, Alick – RHB

b. Droitwich, 15 December 1907; d. Kidderminster, 28 November 1980.

Debut 1927 v Glam., Kidderminster. 1 match for W (amateur) 1927; scored 3 in only innings.

Birmingham League cricket for Kidderminster.

Y

YARDLEY, Thomas James ('Jim') – LHB RM occ. WK
b. Chaddesley Corbett, 27 October 1946. Educated at King Charles I
Grammar School.
 Debut 1967 v Notts., Worcester 1967. 153 matches for W 1967–75 (cap
1972). Highest score: W 135 v Notts., Worcester 1973. 1066 runs (30.45)
in 1971.
 107 matches for Northants 1976–82 (cap 1978). 8287 first-class runs
(25.82).
 Birmingham League cricket for Kidderminster.

YARNOLD, Henry 'Hugo' – RHB WK
b. Worcester, 8 July 1917; d. in road traffic accident, Leamington Spa,
War., 13 August 1974.

T.J. Yardley

H. Yarnold

D.M. Young

M. Younis Ahmed

Debut 1938 v Notts., Trent Bridge. 283 matches for W 1938–55 (professional – cap 1947). Benefit £2,700) 1954. Highest score: W 64 v Sussex, Hove 1946. Holds W record with 104 dismissals (59 ct, 45 st) in a season, 1949. Also dismissed 95 (59 ct, 36 st) in 1951 and 94 (62 ct, 32 st) in 1950. Holds county record for all first-class cricket with 7 dismissals (1 ct, 6 st) in innings, v Scotland, Broughty Ferry 1951. 6 stumpings in innings is world record. Equalled County Championship match record with 6 dismissals (3 ct, 3 st) in innings v Hants, Worcester 1949. 9 dismissals in match (5 ct, 4 st) v Hants, Worcester 1949 – county record until equalled by S.J. Rhodes in 1988. 8 dismissals in match on three other occasions, v Kent, Dover 1949; v Scotland, Broughty Ferry 1951; v Cambridge U, Worcester 1950. 684 dismissals in career (458 ct 226 st) – W record until beaten by R. Booth.

On first-class umpires' list 1959–74.

YOUNG, Douglas Martin – RHB SRA
b. Coalville, Leics., 15 April 1924.

Debut 1946 v India, Worcester. 31 matches for W (professional) 1946–48. Highest score: W 90 v Cambridge U, Cambridge 1947.

435 matches for Glos. 1949–64 (cap 1950). Benefit (£4,600) 1963. Highest first-class score: 198, Glos. v Oxford U, Oxford 1962. Best first-class bowling: 2–35 Glos. v Surrey, The Oval 1964. Holds county 1st-wicket record for Glos. with R.B. Nichols – 395 v Oxford U, Oxford 1962. 1000 runs (all first-class cricket) 13 times – 2179 (41.11) 1959 best. 24555 first-class runs in career (30.69); 40 centuries.

Sport Reporter for BBC West after retirement; lately cricket commentator in South Africa.

YOUNIS AHMED, Mohammed – LHB LM
b. Jullundur, India, 20 October 1947. Educated at Moslem High School,

Lahore; Government College, Lahore.

Debut 1979 v Som., Worcester. 85 matches for W 1979–83 (cap 1979). Highest score: W 221* v Notts., Trent Bridge 1979 (new record for 4th wicket of 281 with J.A. Ormrod during this innings). Best bowling: W 3–33 v Oxford U, Oxford 1979. 1000 runs (4) – 1637 (52.80) 1981 best.

262 matches for Surrey 1965–78 (cap 1969). Also 58 matches for Glam. 1984–86. Played domestic first-class cricket in Pakistan 1961–70, and again in 1987/88, after ban due to South African connections had been lifted. 6 matches for South Australia 1972/73. 4 tests for Pakistan, 1969/70 and again in 1986/87 for that country after a record break. Highest test score: 62 v New Zealand, Karachi 1969/70; 177 test runs (29.50). Best first-class bowling: 4–10, Surrey v Cambridge U, Cambridge 1975. Scored 1000 runs or more (all first-class matches) in England on 12 occasions. County career with W curtailed for disciplinary reasons and disagreement about behavioural policies.

Half-brother Saeed Ahmed (Pakistan).

2

First-class Career and Competition Statistics

First-Class Careers

Player	Inns	N.O.	Runs	H.S.	Av'ge	100s	Runs	Wkts	Av'ge
Abbott, J.D.	5	0	63	42	12.60	—			
Abell, G.E.B.	58	7	1290	131	25.29	2	4	0	—
Adshead, F.H.	3	0	26	14	8.66	—			
Ahl, F.D.	53	3	592	43	11.84	—	384	13	29.53
Ainsley, J.	25	16	64	13	7.11	—			
Ainsworth, M.L.Y.	28	1	854	100	31.62	1	15	0	—
Aldridge, K.J.	100	30	459	24*	6.55	—	5519	241	22.90
Allchurch, T.	6	0	74	51	12.33	—	280	10	28.00
Alleyne, H.L.	41	8	398	72	12.06	—	3222	119	27.07
Anton, J.H.H.	7	0	74	26	10.57	—			
Archer, A.G.	8	0	34	12	4.25	—			
Argent, E.	4	1	22	19	7.33	—	63	0	—
Arnold, E.G.	527	54	14825	215	31.34	24	21411	902	23.73
Ashman, J.R.	40	14	149	24	5.73	—	2430	57	42.63
Ashton, G.	44	0	773	125	17.56	1	43	1	—
Austin, H.	4	0	22	9	5.50	—	56	1	—
Bache, H.G.	25	1	222	36	9.25	—	33	3	11.00
Baker, E.S.	44	19	160	21*	6.40	—			
Baker, H.F.	4	1	21	8*	7.00	—	66	0	—
Baker, W.	4	0	24	7	6.00	—	38	1	—
Bale, E.W.	217	79	1096	43	7.94	—	217	8	27.12
Banks, D.A.	29	3	691	100	26.57	1	17	0	—
Bannister, A.F.	62	16	354	44	7.69	—	2175	92	23.64
Barker, A.R.P.	43	3	544	67	13.60	—			
Barley, J.C.	2	1	1	1*	—	—			
Barnie-Adshead, W.E.	22	1	244	51	11.61	—			
Barrett, B.J.	—	—	—	—	—	—	40	1	—
Baylis, K.R.	7	1	89	26	14.83	—	495	14	35.35
Bayliss, E.G.	2	0	0	0	0.00	—			
Bennett, E.H.	6	0	24	10	4.00	—			
Bennett, M.	2	0	10	8	5.00	—			
Bent, P.	29	1	655	144	23.39	1			
Berkeley, R.G.W.	7	0	37	16	5.28	—			
Berry, R.	118	40	601	32	7.70	—	6263	250	25.05
Bevins, S.R.	2	1	11	6*	—	—			
Bird, A.	225	63	1951	64*	12.04	—	7393	292	25.31
Bird, R.E.	317	31	7442	158*	26.02	7	1110	23	48.26
Birkenshaw, J.	10	0	165	54	16.50	—	644	11	58.54
Blakey, G.M.	4	1	46	42	15.33	—	87	0	—
Blewitt, C.P.	2	0	7	4	3.50	—			
Blunt, L.	19	5	109	18	7.78	—	885	33	26.81
Booth, R.	594	107	9360	113*	19.21	2	3	0	—
Botham, I.T.	38	2	741	126*	20.58	1	1751	68	25.75
Bowles, J.J.	102	14	1155	73	13.12	—	2999	72	41.65
Bowley, F.L.	722	24	20751	276	29.72	38	101	4	25.25
Boyns, C.N.	46	7	778	95	19.94	—	1617	36	44.91
Bradley, M.E.	9	7	9	6*	4.50	—	867	23	37.69
Brain, B.M.	157	41	807	38	6.95	—	12298	508	24.20
Brinton, P.R.	1	0	1	1	—	—			
Brinton, R.L.	4	0	22	10	5.50	—	22	0	—

Player	Inns	N.O.	Runs	H.S.	Av'ge	100s	Runs	Wkts	Av'ge
Brinton, R.S.	24	7	332	72*	19.52	—	13	0	—
Broadbent, R.G.	520	56	12800	155	27.58	13	382	4	95.50
Bromley-Martin, E.G.	13	1	171	39	14.25	—	274	10	27.40
Bromley-Martin, G.E.	56	0	1106	129	19.75	1	72	1	—
Brook, G.W.	218	17	1877	56	9.33	—	12841	461	27.85
Brown, A.	—	—	—	—	—	—			
Brownell, E.L.D.	2	0	28	21	14.00	—			
Bryant, E.H.	30	0	329	63	10.96	—			
Bull, C.H.	302	20	6768	161	24.00	5	56	0	—
Buller, J.S.	168	43	1732	64	13.85	—			
Bullock, M.	6	0	59	27	9.83	—			
Bullock, P.G.	5	0	11	9	2.20	—			
Bunting, E.L.	2	0	1	1	0.50	—			
Burlton, A.T.	10	1	114	35*	12.66	—	38	0	—
Burns, W.B.	335	20	8688	196	27.58	12	5752	187	30.75
Burr, F.B.	2	1	46	39	—	—			
Burrows, R.D.	436	65	5223	112	14.07	2	23604	894	26.40
Busher, S.E.	7	1	32	18*	5.33	—	288	19	15.15
Byrne, G.R.	8	0	28	18	3.50	—	155	1	—
Caldwell, W.S.	33	1	673	133	21.03	2	40	2	20.0
Carmichael, E.G.M.	2	0	6	5	3.00	—			
Carr, A.M.	10	0	150	82	15.00	—	10	0	—
Carter, R.G.M.	163	94	317	23	4.59	—	13630	521	26.16
Cass, G.R.	144	22	2572	172*	21.08	1			
Cave-Rogers, R.A.	1	0	3	3	—	—	25	0	—
Chadd, J.E.	1	0	4	4	—	—	98	2	49.00
Chatham, C.H.	2	0	12	8	6.00	—	65	1	—
Chester, F.	90	17	1768	178*	24.21	4	2493	80	31.16
Chesterton, G.H.	69	21	353	23	7.35	—	4339	168	25.82
Clare, T.	4	0	63	34	15.75	—			
Cliff, A.T.	74	2	986	81*	13.69	—	410	8	51.25
Cobham, Lord	6	1	63	30	12.60	—			
Coldwell, L.J.	333	92	1446	37	6.00	—	21490	1029	20.88
Collier, C.G.A.	85	8	982	72	12.75	—	341	7	48.71
Collinson, J.	2	0	24	23	12.00	—			
Conway, A.J.	49	14	157	20*	4.48	—	1904	53	35.92
Cooper, E.	442	28	13213	216*	31.91	18	44	0	—
Cooper, F.	74	11	1204	113*	19.11	1	30	0	—
Corbett, P.T.	13	3	57	20	5.70	—	77	0	—
Corden, C.F.	33	4	479	64	16.51	—			
Coventry, J.B.	133	13	1774	86	14.78	—	733	16	45.81
Cox, G.C.	4	0	28	19	7.00	—			
Crawley, L.G.	9	0	602	161	66.88	2			
Crisp, R.J.	13	3	107	29	10.70	—	993	42	23.64
Crowe, G.L.	38	2	584	78	16.22	—	35	2	17.50
Cuffe, J.A.	357	32	7404	145	22.78	4	18273	716	25.52
Cumbes, J.	92	43	384	43	7.83	—	7902	246	32.12
Curtis, T.S.	271	35	9363	156	39.67	16	230	4	57.50
Darks, G.C.	8	3	89	39	17.80	—	452	13	34.76
Davidge, G.M.C.	1	0	0	0	—	—			
Davies, T.E.	30	5	481	76	19.24	—	169	6	28.16
Davis, J.P.	8	1	48	38*	6.85	—	45	0	—
Davis, M.	2	0	35	29	17.50	—			
Days, J.E.	3	0	8	5	2.66	—	42	2	21.00
Devereux, L.N.	129	21	2070	81*	19.16	—	4497	106	42.42
Devereux, R.J.	16	3	216	55*	16.61	—	581	13	44.69
Dews, G.	638	53	16671	145	28.49	20	202	2	101.00
Dilley, G.R.	26	12	217	36	15.50	—	2244	110	20.40
D'Oliveira, B.L.	435	65	14120	227	38.16	31	11103	445	24.95
D'Oliveira, D.B.	250	17	6174	146*	26.49	6	923	23	40.13
Dorrell, P.G.	1	1	1	1	—	—			
Duff, A.R.	8	2	79	50*	13.16	—	284	14	20.28

Player	Inns	N.O.	Runs	H.S.	Av'ge	100s	Runs	Wkts	Av'ge
Eden, E.	2	1	27	18*	—	—			
Edwards, H.C.	2	0	11	10	5.50	—			
Ellcock, R.M.	35	11	335	45*	13.95	—	2391	71	33.67
Elliott, J.W.	11	3	66	18*	8.25	—			
Evans, P.S.	9	3	15	5	2.50	—	199	3	66.33
Evans, W.H.B.	9	2	217	107	31.00	1	185	3	61.66
Everitt, R.S.	2	1	6	6*	—	—			
Evers, R.D.M.	26	1	383	60*	15.32	—			
Farnfield, P.H.	1	0	0	0	—	—			
Fawcus, C.L.D.	2	0	47	43	23.50	—	6	0	—
Fearnley, C.D.	174	14	3294	112	20.58	1	37	1	—
Fereday, J.B.	19	0	211	37	11.10	—	103	2	51.50
Fiddian-Green, C.A.F.	36	0	956	108	26.55	1	20	0	—
Field, F.	4	2	26	12	13.00	—	116	4	29.00
Fisher, P.B.	18	8	114	28*	11.40	—			
Flavell, J.A.	444	138	1984	54	6.48	—	32120	1507	21.31
Foley, H.T.H.	2	1	6	6	—	—			
Foster, B.S.	11	0	94	36	8.54	—	29	0	—
Foster, C.K.	5	2	34	16*	11.33	—			
Foster, G.N.	144	13	4114	175	31.40	7	48	2	24.00
Foster, H.K.	441	15	15053	216	35.33	28	349	11	31.72
Foster, M.K.	276	8	7876	158	29.38	12	256	3	85.33
Foster, N.J.A.	14	4	219	40*	21.90	—			
Foster, R.E.	136	9	5699	246*	44.87	13	1004	21	47.80
Foster, W.L.	51	2	1600	172*	32.65	3	13	0	—
Fowler, R.H.	7	1	72	35	12.00	—	105	7	15.00
Fox, J.	159	16	2438	73	17.04	—	1285	31	41.45
Fox, W.V.	281	31	6654	198	26.61	11	137	2	68.50
Francis, P.T.	5	1	95	66	23.75	—			
Fulton, H.A.	1	1	2	2*	—	—			
Gales, L.E.	26	6	155	19	7.75	—	394	10	39.40
Garratt, H.S.	9	0	111	39	12.33	—			
Gaukrodger, G.W.	177	45	2230	91	16.89	—			
Genders, W.R.	9	3	154	55*	25.66	—	70	3	23.33
Gethin, S.J.	7	0	86	41	12.28	—	49	1	—
Gethin, W.G.	2	0	20	19	10.00	—			
Gibbons, H.H.I.H.	666	57	20918	212*	34.34	44	737	7	105.28
Gifford, N.	619	189	5848	89	13.60	—	36071	1615	22.33
Gilbert, H.A.	111	35	538	31*	7.07	—	6973	249	28.00
Good, D.C.	2	1	7	6*	—	—	75	1	—
Goodreds, W.A.	1	1	4	4*	—	—	48	0	—
Gordon, H.P.	13	1	157	68*	13.08	—			
Graveney, T.W.	347	62	13160	166	46.17	27	182	4	45.50
Greenstock, J.W.	22	4	124	23*	6.88	—	875	23	38.04
Greenstock, W.	7	0	86	33	12.28	—	26	0	—
Greenwood, L.W.	4	0	33	25	8.25	—			
Greig, G.G.F.	34	8	215	37	8.26	—	1220	31	39.35
Griffith, K.	61	8	795	59	15.00	—	1753	50	35.06
Griffiths, G.C.	10	0	42	16	4.20	—			
Grimshaw, V.	32	2	418	103	13.93	1	46	2	23.00
Grisewood, F.H.	2	1	7	6*	—	—			
Grove, C.W.	20	1	180	25	9.47	—	1275	42	30.35
Hall, B.C.	4	1	34	21	11.33	—	97	3	32.33
Hampton, W.M.	24	1	298	57	12.95	—	13	1	—
Harber, J.	2	0	3	3	1.50	—	46	3	15.33
Harkness, D.P.	19	0	488	163	25.68	1	274	6	45.66
Harper, H.	2	0	10	7	5.00	—			
Harris, G.C.	8	3	6	4	1.20	—	120	2	60.00
Harrison, C.S.	29	2	166	28	6.14	—	1043	25	41.72
Harry, F.	11	2	77	14*	8.55	—	294	8	36.75
Hartill, W.N.	1	0	2	2	—	—			
Headley, R.G.A.	725	60	20712	187	31.14	32	568	12	47.33

Player	Inns	N.O.	Runs	H.S.	Av'ge	100s	Runs	Wkts	Av'ge
Hemsley, E.J.O.	389	57	9740	176*	29.33	8	2497	70	35.67
Henderson, S.P.	36	4	467	64	14.59	—	46	0	
Hick, G.A.	165	18	9071	405*	61.70	32	2604	80	32.55
Hickton, W.H.	9	0	41	17	4.55	—	104	2	52.00
Higgins, H.L.	181	13	3437	137*	20.45	4			
Higgins, J.B.	204	10	3837	123	19.77	3	1339	28	47.82
Higginson, J.G.	1	1	0	0*	—	—	20	0	—
Higgs–Walker, J.A.	3	1	44	44	22.00	—	89	1	—
Hill, D.V.	46	7	405	38	10.38	—	2321	78	29.75
Hill, W.H.	4	1	46	13*	15.33	—			
Holder, V.A.	196	51	1553	52	10.71	—	13530	586	23.08
Holyoake, R.H.	6	0	47	22	7.83	—			
Hopkins, H.O.	114	5	2257	137	20.70	2	190	4	47.50
Horton, H.	19	3	129	21	8.06	—	32	0	—
Horton, J.	103	12	1258	70	13.82	—	362	5	72.40
Horton, M.J.	665	47	17974	233	29.04	22	20381	774	26.33
Howard, J.	10	0	85	28	8.50	—			
Howorth, R.	571	50	10538	114	20.22	3	27218	1274	21.36
Hughes, N.	32	6	651	95	25.03	—	317	10	31.70
Hughes, R.C.	10	2	47	21	5.87	—	695	15	46.26
Human, R.H.C.	62	4	1540	81	26.55	—	601	10	60.10
Humpherson, V.W.	25	5	154	16	7.70	—	500	16	31.25
Humphries, C.A.	24	3	328	44	15.61	—			
Humphries, D.J.	243	43	4969	133*	24.84	4			
Humphries, G.H.	3	0	66	36	22.00	—	13	0	—
Humphries, N.H.	11	1	137	22	13.70	—	52	0	—
Hunt, F.H.	87	18	774	40*	11.21	—	1463	44	33.25
Hussain, M.	1	0	4	4	—	—			
Hutchings, W.E.C.	39	3	814	85	22.61	—			
Illingworth, R.K.	173	46	2351	120*	18.51	1	10478	320	32.74
Imran Khan	67	6	1518	166	24.88	4	3150	128	24.60
Inchmore, J.D.	243	53	3137	113	16.51	1	14546	503	29.91
Isaac, A.W.	87	5	1106	60	13.48	—			
Isaac, H.W.	3	0	32	23	10.66	—	32	0	—
Isaac, J.E.V.	3	0	19	10	6.33	—			
Isles, D.	1	1	17	17*	—	—			
Jackson, J.F.C.	2	0	6	6	3.00	—			
Jackson, P.F.	546	207	2044	40	6.04	—	30209	1139	26.52
Jagger, S.T.	9	0	74	41	8.22	—	196	7	28.00
Jeavons, E.P.	2	1	1	1*	—	—			
Jenkins, R.O.	530	109	9215	109	21.88	1	27240	1148	23.72
Jewell, A.N.	43	0	864	128	20.09	3			
Jewell, J.M.H.	4	0	30	24	7.50	-			
Jewell, M.F.S.	220	14	3906	125	18.96	2	3217	98	32.82
Jobson, E.P.	12	0	162	26	13.50	—	8	0	—
Johnson, I.N.	43	10	716	69	21.69	—	1533	37	41.43
Jolly, N.W.	2	1	9	8	—	—			
Jones, B.J.R.	81	3	1076	65	13.79	—			
Jones, R.	2	0	25	23	12.50	—			
Kapil Dev, N.	40	6	1456	100	42.82	1	1624	72	22.55
Keene, J.W.	32	9	107	12	4.65	-	1312	62	21.16
Kenyon, D.	1060	51	34490	259	34.18	70	178	1	—
Kimber, S.J.S	1	1	14	14*	—	—	72	3	24.00
Kimpton, R.C.M.	25	1	695	106	28.95	1	71	2	35.50
King, B.P.	140	6	2619	124	19.54	4	4	0	—
King, C.L.	3	0	158	123	52.66	1	39	1	—
King, J.W.	73	12	1015	91	16.63	—			
Krikken, B.E.	1	0	4	4	—	—			
Lampitt, S.R.	23	6	221	46	13.00	—	821	34	24.14
Lanchbury, R.J.	13	3	245	50*	24.50	—			
Lane, A.F.	76	8	1163	76	17.10	—	1218	23	52.95

Player	Inns	N.O.	Runs	H.S.	Av'ge	100s	Runs	Wkts	Av'ge
Lang, J.M.	14	8	27	9*	4.50	—	412	8	51.50
Larkham, W.T.	2	0	13	13	6.50	—	64	1	—
Leatherdale, D.A.	23	2	348	34*	16.57	—	20	1	—
Leeson, P.G.	2	0	7	7	3.50	—			
Legard, A.R.	2	0	22	18	11.00	—	31	0	—
Lister, J.	37	4	750	99	22.72	—			
Lobban, H.W.	23	11	81	18	6.75	—	1452	47	30.89
Lord, G.J.	68	6	1477	101	23.82	1	24	0	—
Lowe, W.W.	65	5	1328	154	22.13	4	950	28	33.92
Lyttelton, C.F.	12	2	67	18*	6.70	—	510	19	26.84
Lyttelton, C.J.	152	14	2708	162	19.62	1	1250	32	39.06
McEvoy, M.S.A.	39	1	757	103	19.92	1			
McEwan, S.M.	23	11	184	28*	15.33	—	2880	101	28.51
Maclean, J.F.	79	7	1163	121	16.15	1			
Mann, W.H.	2	0	7	4	3.50	—			
Martin, E.G.	5	1	35	18*	8.75	—	136	2	68.00
Martin, S.H.	405	26	9993	191*	26.36	13	13358	458	29.16
Maxwell, C.R.N.	9	0	138	31	15.33	—			
Mills, G.T.	4	0	46	23	11.50	—			
Mitchell, K.J.	2	0	10	10	5.00	—			
Moores, P.	15	3	215	45	17.91	—			
Morris, P.J.	2	0	74	71	37.00	—	13	0	—
Morris, R.	3	0	7	7	2.33	—			
Mortimer, H.	2	0	11	7	5.50	—			
Moss, R.H.	2	0	2	2	1.00	—	5	1	—
Moule, H.G.	2	0	102	57	51.00	—			
Munn, R.G.	1	0	2	2	—	—			
Murray Willis, P.G.	12	0	80	20	6.66	—			
Naden, J.R.	3	2	23	16*	—	—	136	2	68.00
Neale, P.A.	512	76	15889	167	36.44	26	283	1	—
Nesbitt, A.S.	2	1	5	3	—				
Nesfield, E.R.	4	0	27	16	6.75	—	10	0	
Neville, B.P.	9	2	61	17*	8.71	—	148	7	21.14
Newport, P.J.	122	43	1969	77*	24.92	—	8651	328	26.37
Nichol, M.	233	16	7480	262*	34.47	17	1281	21	61.00
Nichols, J.E.	9	1	39	13	4.87	—	13	0	—
Norton, E.W.	10	3	82	23	11.71	—	338	7	48.28
Oakley, L.	13	4	43	11	4.77	—	393	12	32.75
Ormrod, J.A.	789	91	21753	204*	31.16	31	1064	25	42.56
O'Shaughnessy, S.J.	20	1	153	44	8.05	—	161	4	40.25
Outschoorn, L.	586	53	15257	215*	28.62	35	1961	33	59.42
Palmer, Cecil, H.	2	1	116	75*	—	—			
Palmer, Charles, H.	114	7	3252	177	30.39	6	1844	49	37.63
Parker, J.M.	103	9	3315	140	35.36	6	188	4	47.00
Passey, M.F.W.	1	0	1	1	—	—	57	1	—
Pataudi, Nawab of	64	7	2860	231*	50.17	8	239	2	119.50
Patel, D.N.	364	31	9734	197	29.23	16	13089	357	36.66
Patel, H.V.	1	0	39	39	—	—			
Pawson, A.G.	2	1	12	12	—	—			
Pearson, D.B.	104	21	712	49	8.57	—	5347	202	26.47
Pearson, F.A.	794	37	18496	167	24.43	22	24208	815	29.70
Perks, R.T.D.	841	142	8485	75	12.13	—	50857	2143	23.73
Perry, E.H.	16	0	148	46	9.25	—	732	22	33.27
Perry, H.	8	1	109	40	15.57	—	46	1	—
Perryman, S.P.	33	16	127	22	7.47	—	1966	49	40.12
Phelps, P.H.	4	0	25	11	6.25	—			
Ponsonby, C.B.	127	26	784	50*	7.76	—			
Porthouse, S.C.	8	1	70	27	10.00	—	4	0	—
Powell, A.J.	2	0	10	9	5.00	—	8	0	—
Powys-Keck, H.J.	5	1	32	25	8.00	—	149	4	37.25
Pratt, D.	12	6	10	3*	1.66	—	546	13	42.00

Player	Inns	N.O.	Runs	H.S.	Av'ge	100s	Runs	Wkts	Av'ge
Preece, C.R.	160	23	1575	69	11.49	—	4037	135	29.90
Price, J.	18	4	81	33	5.78	—	611	12	50.91
Price, W.H.	1	1	0	0*	—	—	12	0	—
Price, W.L.	3	0	12	7	4.00	—	284	8	35.50
Pridgeon, A.P.	221	84	1188	67	8.67	—	17367	530	32.76
Pullan, C.D.A.	41	6	768	84	20.75	—	192	5	38.40
Quaife, B.W.	447	42	8498	136*	20.98	3	231	5	46.20
Radford, N.V.	95	21	1193	66*	16.12	—	10202	434	23.50
Rhodes, S.J.	156	53	2811	108	27.29	1	—		
Richardson, D.W.	638	61	15843	169	27.45	16	322	8	40.25
Richardson, P.E.	286	20	9118	185	34.27	15	178	1	—
Richardson, W.E.	57	17	269	24	6.72	—	1865	44	42.38
Righton, E.G. (senior)	4	0	60	48	15.00	—	21	1	—
Righton, E.G. (junior)	7	0	27	19	3.85	—			
Riley, J.	1	0	1	1	—	—	48	3	16.00
Roberts, C.P.	1	1	0	0*	—	40	1	—	
Roberts, E.S.	6	0	23	12	3.83	—			
Robinson, A.E.	11	1	95	37	9.50	—			
Robinson, P.J.	5	0	49	37	9.80	—	132	6	22.00
Robson, C.G.W.	4	0	103	46	25.75	—			
Rogers, H.O.	146	31	1683	118*	14.63	1	3705	138	26.84
Romney, F.W.	7	3	39	20*	9.75	—			
Root, C.F.	470	38	6772	107	15.67	1	28465	1387	20.52
Rose, T.G.	10	1	47	15	5.22	—	219	7	31.28
Rudge, L.M.	1	0	1	1	—	—	36	0	—
Rumsey, F.E.	16	2	166	43	11.85	—	661	31	21.32
Rutherford, I.A.	3	0	9	8	3.00	—	15	1	—
Sale, H.G.	8	3	74	28*	14.80	—	·		
Sanderson, G.B.	1	0	16	16	—	—			
Santall, J.F.E.	13	1	117	36*	9.75	—	124	2	62.00
Saunders, M.	2	0	12	12	6.00	—	212	6	35.33
Scholey, J.C.	7	2	32	16	6.40	—			
Scothern, M.G.	—	—	—	—	—	—	42	1	—
Scott, M.S.	60	3	1383	109	24.26	1	37	0	—
Sedgley, J.B.	27	2	389	95	15.56	—			
Seeley, G.H.	1	0	7	7	—	—			
Senghera, R.	25	7	281	36*	15.61	—	2179	57	38.22
Serrurier, L.R.	10	2	279	110	34.87	1	267	7	38.14
Shakespeare, W.H.N.	44	4	789	67*	19,72	—	8	0	—
Shepherd, S.G.	2	0	9	9	4.50	—	4	0	—
Sheppard, G.A.	4	0	18	11	4.50	—			
Sheppard, T.W.	2	0	36	22	18.00	—			
Shorting, W.L.	17	1	165	27	10.31	—			
Shutt, A.	—	—	—	—	—	—	181	2	90.50
Simpson–Hayward, GHT	253	24	4335	130	18.93	3	8099	362	22.37
Singleton, A.P.	100	11	2848	164	32.00	4	2614	70	37.34
Singleton, G.M.	4	0	31	23	7.75	—	91	4	22.75
Slade, D.N.F.	376	98	5021	125	18.06	1	10761	469	22.94
Smith, D.J.	15	0	114	29	7.60	—			
Smith, D.M.	87	13	3247	189*	43.87	8	57	3	19.00
Smith, E.S.	4	0	33	22	8.25	—			
Smith, J.C.	27	1	313	70	12.03	—	10	0	—
Smith, L.K.	7	1	62	28	10.33	—	20	1	—
Solly, E.W.	10	1	78	43	8.66	—	665	14	47.50
Somers, Lord	28	1	377	52	13.96	—	4	0	—
Southall, H.	1	0	11	11	—	—			
Spencer, A.H.	52	1	934	85	18.31	—	23	0	—
Spencer, H.N.E.	2	0	28	26	14.00	—	68	2	34.00
Spilsbury, J.W.E.	1	0	16	16	—	—	86	0	—
Standen, J.A.	175	29	2096	92*	14.35	—	7934	313	25.34
Stanning, J.	11	1	127	56*	12.70	—			
Stephenson, J.W.A.	2	0	20	12	10.00	—	66	1	—

Player	Inns	N.O.	Runs	H.S.	Av'ge	100s	Runs	Wkts	Av'ge
Stevens, B.G.	31	2	364	41	12.55	—	18	0	—
Stewart, D.E.R.	35	3	578	69	18.06	—	72	0	—
Stimpson, P.J.	54	3	1327	103	26.01	1	19	0	—
Straw, T.	94	38	600	32	10.71	—			
Stringer, T.	2	1	0	0*	—	—	103	1	—
Styler, S.W.	31	6	134	24	5.36	—			
Suckling, E.	5	1	85	58	21.25	—	100	4	25.00
Summers, D.W.L.	1	0	4	4	—	—	11	0	—
Summers, F.T.	91	27	409	36	6.39	—			
Sutor, J.A.	2	0	3	2	1.50	—			
Swalwell, R.S.	30	1	409	57	14.10	—	35	0	—
Tarbox, C.V.	398	31	5824	109	15.86	2	13256	375	35.34
Tasker, A.G.E.	—	—	—	—	—	—			
Taylor, R.J.	2	0	1	1	0.50	—	41	0	—
Taylor, W.H.	189	39	1733	59*	11.55	—	5673	159	35.67
Thomas, W.R.K.	2	1	57	44	—	—	54	0	—
Thornycroft, G.M.	2	0	3	3	1.50	—			
Thorp, P.	4	0	19	11	4.75	—			
Thursfield, J.H.	6	0	70	35	11.66	—			
Tinkler, E.	2	0	8	7	4.00	—	14	0	—
Tipper, B.C.C.	10	1	137	43	15.22	—	80	4	20.00
Tolley, C.M.	6	2	120	37	30.00	—	138	1	—
Tomkinson, F.M.	1	0	0	0	—	—			
Tomkinson, G.S.	3	0	12	10	4.00	—			
Toppin, C.G.	5	0	17	10	3.40	—			
Toppin, J.F.T.	2	0	8	6	4.00	—	5	0	—
Turner, G.M.	493	65	22298	311*	52.09	72	114	5	22.80
Turner, J.W.C.	87	3	1215	106	14.46	1	32	2	16.00
Turner, R.E.	96	8	1010	66	11..47	—	225	4	56.25
Vorster, L.P.	1	1	16	16*	—	—			
Wakefield, P.H.	2	0	8	8	4.00	—	13	0	—
Wakelin, E.	1	0	6	6	—	—			
Walford, J.E.S.	12	0	145	31	12.08	—	67	1	—
Wallace, C.W.	7	1	66	39*	11.00	—			
Walters, C.F.	237	20	8193	226	37.75	18	335	5	67.00
Warne, F.B.	141	12	2670	115	20.69	2	3481	96	36.26
Warner, A.E.,	39	9	480	67	16.00	—	1947	61	31.91
Watkins, S.G.	2	0	105	77	52.50	—			
Watson, G.G.	35	6	341	38	11.75	—	2360	70	33.71
Webster, A.J.	11	5	81	25	13.50	—	734	15	48.93
Wells, T.U.	2	0	9	9	4.50	—			
Weston, M.J.	229	19	5189	145*	24.70	3	2924	77	37.97
Wheldon, G.F.	244	25	4938	112	22.54	3	77	0	—
Whitcombe, P.J.	10	3	241	89*	34.42	—			
White, A.F.T.	188	12	3745	95	21.27	—	26	0	—
White, M.E.	46	12	238	37	7.00	—	2076	66	31.45
Whitehead, J.P.	46	9	741	71	20.02	—	1384	35	39.54
Whiting, N.H.	96	11	1583	118	18.62	2	657	13	50.53
Wilcock, H.G.	137	31	1697	74	16.01	—	3	0	—
Wilkes, A.J.	22	2	113	25	5.65	—			
Wilkes, W.H.W.	25	1	419	109	17.45	1			
Wilkinson, J.W.	2	2	4	4*	—	—	45	1	—
Wilkinson, K.W.	77	11	1657	141	25.10	2	1551	48	32.31
Williams, H.	6	3	7	4	2.33	—	185	2	92.50
Williams, R.H.	68	4	713	81	11.14	—			
Wilson, G.A.	229	37	2202	78	11.46	—	17129	719	23.82
Wilson, G.C.	119	34	609	40	7.16	—	4049	150	26.99
Wilson, G.T.O.	16	7	10	4*	1.11	—	1000	18	55.55
Wilson, H.	11	3	64	21	8.00	—	373	13	28.69
Winnington, J.F.S.	2	0	20	20	10.00	—			
Winwood, T.L.	30	4	404	104	15.53	1	10	0	—
Wright, L.	348	18	6593	134	19.97	5	3649	76	48.01

Player	Inns	N.O.	Runs	H.S.	Av'ge	100s	Runs	Wkts	Av'ge
Wyatt, R.E.S.	138	13	4233	166*	33.86	6	2387	62	38.50
Wyers, A.	1	0	3	3	—	—			
Yardley, T.J.	232	40	4865	135	25.33	4	14	0	—
Yarnold, H.	409	68	3620	64	10.61	—			
Young, D.M.	47	7	766	90	19.15	—	0	0	—
Younis Ahmed, M.	133	30	5486	221*	53.26	13	521	12	43.41

Gillette Cup and Nat-West Trophy

Player	Inns	N.O.	Runs	H.S.	Av'ge	100s	Runs	Wkts	Av'ge	Runs/ Over	B.B.
Alleyne, H.L.	2	1	24	19	—	—	59	4	14.75	2.68	3/27
Banks, D.A.	1	1	11	11*	—	—					
Booth, R.	11	1	150	55	15.00	—					
Botham, I.T.	3	0	154	101	51.33	1	186	12	15.50	3.96	5/51
Boyns, C.N.	2	0	5	5	2.50	—	36	3	12.00	3.60	3/36
Brain, B.M.	14	8	109	21*	18.17	—	534	28	19.07	2.81	4/13
Broadbent, R.G.	3	0	64	51	21.33	—					
Carter, R.G.M.	3	1	9	5*	4.50	—	312	8	39.00	3.66	2/20
Cass, G.R.	10	1	183	43*	20.33	—					
Coldwell, L.J.	8	5	24	8	8.00	—	330	17	19.41	2.79	4/39
Cumbes, J.	4	2	12	6	6.00	—	266	13	20.46	3.13	4/23
Curtis, T.S.	22	3	966	120	50.84	1	15	2	7.50	3.75	1/6
Devereux, R.J.	1	0	30	30	—	—	24	0	—	4.00	—
Dilley, G.R.	3	1	28	25	14.00	—	276	14	19.71	3.25	5/29
D'Oliveira, B.L.	26	2	610	102	25.42	1	783	37	21.16	2.79	4/18
D'Oliveira, D.B.	16	1	359	99	23.93	—	134	6	22.33	3.53	2/28
Ellcock, R.M.	1	0	6	6	—	—	49	3	16.33	4.90	3/49
Fearnley, C.D.	2	0	7	7	3.50	—					
Flavell, J.A.	8	3	18	9	3.60	—	322	33	9.76	2.47	6/14
Gifford, N.	27	4	202	38	8.78	—	1017	39	26.07	2.93	4/7
Graveney, T.W.	14	3	534	93	48.54	—					
Griffith, K.	—	—	—	—	—	—					
Headley, R.G.A.	24	1	575	83	25.00	—					
Hemsley, E.J.O.	17	1	274	73	17.12	—	180	4	45.00	4.27	2/17
Henderson, S.P.	2	0	50	33	25.00	—					
Hick, G.A.	15	2	788	172*	60,61	3	225	9	25.00	3.38	4/54
Holder, V.A.	14	5	79	25*	8.77	—	604	22	27.45	3.06	3/14
Horton, M.J.	9	1	278	114	34.75	1	142	7	20.29	2.51	2/20
Humphries, D.J.	10	1	178	53	19.33	—					
Illingworth, R.K.	7	2	48	22	9.60	—	460	15	30.66	3.06	4/20
Imran Khan	6	1	120	55*	24.00	—	235	3	78.33	3.80	2/24
Inchmore, J.D.	15	4	118	32*	10.72	—	842	37	22.75	3.46	5/25
Johnson, I.N.	1	0	23	23	—	—	30	3	10.00	3.15	3/30
Kapil Dev	4	1	48	38*	16.00	—	162	8	20.25	2.95	5/52
Kenyon, D.	10	0	118	42	11.80	—					
King, C.L.	1	0	11	11	—	—	36	1	—	4.50	1/36
Lampitt, S.R.	2	1	9	9*	—	—	114	4	28.50	4.07	2/35
Leatherdale, D.A.	6	1	94	43	18.80	—					
Lord, G.J.	1	0	0	0	—	—					
McEwan, S.M.	1	0	6	6	—	—	51	3	17.00	4.64	3/51

Player	Inns	N.O.	Runs	H.S.	Av'ge	100s	Runs	Wkts	Av'ge	Runs/ Over	B.B.
Neale, P.A.	29	3	901	98	34.65	—					
Newport, P.J.	7	2	60	25	12.00	—	400	12	33.33	3.17	3/62
Ormrod, J.A.	31	2	634	59	21.86	—					
O'Shaughnessy, S.J.	4	0	122	62	30.50	—	29	0	—	4.14	
Parker, J.M.	7	0	286	107	40.86	1					
Patel, D.N.	16	2	309	54	22.07	—	435	14	31.07	3.34	4/22
Perryman, S.P.	—	—	—	—	—	—	32	0	—		
Pridgeon, A.P.	10	7	38	13*	12.66	—	517	16	32.31	2.95	3/7
Radford, N.V.	8	2	61	37	10.16	—	587	23	25.52	3.20	3/20
Rhodes, S.J.	14	6	152	61	19.00	—	1	0	—	1.00	—
Richardson, D.W.	10	1	121	23	13.44	—					
Scott, M.S.	3	0	61	33	20.33	—					
Shutt, A.	1	1	0	0*	—	—	48	0	—	4.24	—
Slade, D.N.F.	7	1	36	17*	7.20	—	109	9	12.11	2.58	3/21
Smith, D.M.	8	0	395	107	49.37	1	5	1	—	2.50	1/0
Standen, J.A.	2	1	44	31	—	—	80	9	8.88	1.90	5/14
Stimpson, P.J.	2	0	14	8	7.00	—					
Turner, G.M.	22	2	894	117*	44.70	4					
Weston, M.J.	17	4	419	50	32.23	1	390	10	39.00	3.74	4/30
Wilcock, H.G.	4	0	35	16	8.75	—					
Wilkinson, K.W.	3	0	104	95	34.66	—	31	1	—	2.58	1/31
Yardley, T.J.	11	3	228	52*	28.50	—					
Younis Ahmed	5	0	99	44	19.80	—	125	4	31.25	3.68	2/54

Benson & Hedges Cup

Player	Inns	N.O.	Runs	H.S.	Av'ge	100s	Runs	Wkts	Av'ge	Runs/ Over	B.B.
Alleyne, H.L.	6	1	22	10	4.40	—	335	11	30.45	3.16	3/39
Birkenshaw, J.	3	0	20	14	6.66	—	143	2	71.50	4.61	2/54
Botham, I.T.	11	0	160	43	14.54	—	371	24	15.45	3.48	5/41
Boyns, C.N.	5	0	37	15	7.40	—	215	6	35.83	3.41	2/30
Brain, B.M.	9	3	51	12	8.50	—	474	22	21.54	2.78	3/25
Carter, R.G.M.	1	0	0	0	—	—	128	5	25.60	2.98	3/28
Cass, G.R.	11	2	179	56	19.88	—					
Cumbes, J.	12	8	25	7*	6.25	—	639	18	35.50	3.33	3/34
Curtis, T.S.	24	2	705	78	32.04	—					
Dilley, G.R.	4	1	29	16	9.66	—	336	19	17.68	2.96	3/28
D'Oliveira, B.L.	30	4	890	84	34.23	—	794	33	24.06	2.72	4/23
D.Oliveira, D.B.	28	3	593	66	23.72	—	148	5	29.60	3.89	3/12
Gifford, N.	34	9	283	33	11.32	—	1633	67	24.37	3.30	6/8
Griffith, K.	—	—	—	—	—	—	25	0	—		
Headley, R.G.A.	15	0	491	132	32.73	1					
Hemsley, E.J.O.	43	3	845	95	21.12	—	329	10	32.90	3.74	3/30
Hick, G.A.	19	3	867	109	54.18	3	135	3	45.00	4.09	2/25
Holder, V.A.	17	8	67	17*	7.44	—	691	37	18.67	2.90	5/12
Humphries, D.J.	28	4	317	82	13.20	—					
Illingworth, R.K.	11	7	78	17*	19.50	—	598	20	29.90	3.62	4/36
Imran Khan	6	2	237	72	59.25	—	254	9	28.22	3.39	4/36
Inchmore, J.D.	38	12	352	49*	13.53	—	1811	71	25.50	3.46	6/29
Johnson, I.N.	9	1	66	26	8.25	—	297	8	37.12	4.07	2/22

Player	Inns	N.O.	Runs	H.S.	Av'ge	100s	Runs	Wkts	Av'ge	Runs/ Over	B.B.
Jones, B.J.R.	2	2	49	44*	—	—					
Kapil Dev	4	0	54	32	13.50	—	139	3	46.33	3.39	1/6
King, C.,L.	4	0	138	61	34.50	—	61	0	—	2.90	—
Lanchbury, R.J.	—	—	—	—	—	—					
Lord, G.J.	5	0	41	18	8.20	—					
McEvoy, M.S.A.	3	1	50	24	25.00	—					
Neale, P.A.	52	6	1387	125	30.15	1					
Newport, P.J.	12	3	70	15	7.77	—	518	23	22.52	3.36	5/22
Ormrod, J.A.	54	6	1587	124*	33.06	1	29	1	—	4.46	1/23
O'Shaughnessy, S.J.	4	0	38	14	9.50	—	4	0	—	4.00	—
Parker, J.M.	8	0	218	80	27.25	—					
Patel, D.N.	36	4	727	90*	22.71	—	886	29	30.55	3.49	3/42
Perryman, S.P.	2	2	15	10*	—	—	165	7	23.57	4.02	4/28
Pridgeon, A.P.	20	11	81	13*	9.00	—	1683	35	48.08	3.80	3/57
Radford, N.V.	16	9	180	39*	25.71	—	757	33	22.93	3.46	4/25
Rhodes, S.J.	20	5	329	51*	21.93	—					
Senghera, R.	2	0	23	12	11.50	—	32	0	—	5.33	—
Smith, D.M.	14	3	555	126	50.45	1					
Stewart, D.E.R.	3	0	92	38	30.66	—					
Stimpson, P.J.	3	1	13	12	6.50	—					
Turner, G.M.	47	3	1433	143*	32.56	2					
Warner, A.E.	5	2	39	24*	13.00	—	248	8	31.00	3.71	2/26
Watson, G.G.	3	1	10	5*	5.00	—	115	12	9.58	2.63	5/22
Weston, M.J.	29	1	535	56	19.10	—	325	11	29.54	3.60	2/27
Wilcock, H.G.	9	2	110	49*	15.71	—					
Wilkinson, K.W.	7	1	51	19	8.50	—	23	3	7.66	1.92	3/20
Yardley, T.J.	17	5	354	75*	29.50	—					
Younis Ahmed	19	1	575	115	31.94	2	208	9	23.11	4.00	4/37

Sunday League

Player	Inns	N.O.	Runs	H.S.	Av'ge	100s	Runs	Wkts	Av'ge	Runs/ Over	B.B.
Alleyne, H.L.	16	3	152	32	11.69	—	736	31	23.74	3.91	4/24
Banks, D.A.	11	1	91	23	9.10	—					
Barker, A.R.P.	4	1	47	25	15.66	—					
Barrett, B.J.	1	1	5	5*	—	—	43	0	—	5.38	—
Bent, P.	3	0	51	36	17.00	—					
Bevins, S.R.	—	—	—	—	—	—					
Birkenshaw, J.	2	0	21	16	10.50	—	59	3	19.66	3.69	3/17
Booth, R.	1	1	10	10*	—	—					
Botham, I.T.	23	1	888	125*	40.36	1	734	36	20.38	4.70	5/27
Boyns, C.N.	28	5	251	41*	10.91	—	965	27	35.74	4.06	4/34
Brain, B.M.	30	12	93	15	5.17	—	2040	93	21.94	4.20	4/27
Brown, A.	—	—	—	—	—	—					
Carter, R.G.M.	11	9	11	3*	5.50	—	983	49	20.06	3.90	5/27
Cass, G.R.	57	12	960	77	21.33	—					
Coldwell, L.J.	3	1	4	4	2.00	—	133	6	22.16	3.01	3/24
Cumbes, J.	23	14	40	14*	4.44	—	2176	72	30.22	4.20	3/13
Curtis, T.S.	85	13	2755	102	38.26	1					
Dilley, G.R.	1	0	0	0	—	—	481	14	34.35	4.54	3/30

Player	Inns	N.O.	Runs	H.S.	Av'ge	100s	Runs	Wkts	Av'ge	Runs/Over	B.B.
D'Oliveira, B.L.	108	12	2137	100	22.26	1	2706	113	23.95	3.92	5/26
D'Oliveira, D.B.	95	9	2020	103	23.48	1	232	7	33.14	5.95	3/23
Ellcock, R.M.	5	2	6	5*	2.00	—	235	13	18.07	3.83	4/43
Fisher, P.B.	1	1	0	0*	—	—					
Gifford, N.	115	47	782	31	11.50	—	5281	202	26.14	4.39	5/28
Graveney, T.W.	26	3	507	68	22.04	—					
Griffith, K.	8	2	61	16	10.16	—	105	3	35.00	4.38	2/27
Headley, R.G.A.	79	9	2379	112*	33.99	1					
Hemsley, E.J.O.	142	20	2904	77	23.80	—	1692	59	28.67	4.66	4/42
Henderson, S.P.	14	3	130	28	11.81	—					
Hick, G.A.	69	11	2258	111	38.93	1	799	27	29.59	5.36	4/42
Holder, V.A.	61	15	323	35*	7.02	—	2970	176	16.87	3.43	6/33
Humphries, D.J.	87	12	1056	62	14.08	—					
Illingworth, R.K.	39	20	180	22	9.47	—	2178	99	22.00	4.60	5/24
Imran Khan	29	7	793	75	36.05	—	1018	44	23.14	4.15	5/29
Inchmore, J.D.	96	28	992	45	14.58	—	4240	169	25.08	4.25	4/9
Johnson, I.N.	20	2	190	36*	10.56	—	463	14	33.07	3.70	3/21
Jones, B.J.R.	11	1	128	36*	12.80	—					
Kapil Dev	15	0	239	40	15.93	—	501	15	33.40	4.80	3/20
King, C.L.	6	1	317	127	63.40	2	138	1	—	6.00	1/18
Lampitt, S.R.	5	1	45	21	11.25	—	353	13	27.15	5.43	4/30
Lanchbury, R.J.	3	0	25	14	8.33	—					
Leatherdale, D.A.	8	3	146	62*	29.20	—					
Lord, G.J.	1	0	6	6	—	—					
McEvoy, M.S.A.	8	2	105	27*	17.50	—					
Moores, P.	3	3	24	14*	—	—					
Neale, P.A.	186	45	4195	102	29.75	1	50	2	25.00	6.00	2/46
Newport, P.J.	29	12	205	26*	12.05	—	1566	56	27.96	4.60	4/18
Ormrod, J.A.	176	17	3898	110*	24.51	1	105	3	35.00	5.53	3/51
O'Shaughnessy, S.J.	21	3	450	69	25.00	—	344	10	34.40	5.59	2/12
Parker, J.M.	37	3	638	86	18.76	—					
Patel, D.N.	131	11	2523	125	21.02	1	2841	91	31.21	4.90	5/27
Perryman, S.P.	4	3	30	19	—	—	455	16	28.43	5.06	4/31
Pridgeon, A.P.	51	29	148	17	6.72	—	4860	167	29.10	4.48	6/26
Radford, N.V.	40	20	482	41*	24.67	—	2031	96	21.15	4.57	5/32
Rhodes, S.J.	51	12	884	48*	22.66	—					
Roberts, C.P.	—	—	—	—	—	—	32	2	16.00	4.00	2/32
Scott, M.S.	20	0	315	42	15.75	—					
Senghera, R.	3	1	17	10	8.50	—	151	2	75.50	4.98	1/37
Shutt, A.	2	0	0	0	0.00	—	96	2	48.00	4.00	2/25
Slade, D.N.F.	24	5	232	41*	12.21	—	232	10	23.20	4.32	2/2
Smith, D.M.	30	7	697	66*	30.30	—					
Smith, L.K.	1	0	3	3	—	—					
Standen, J.A.	19	5	155	29	11.07	—	604	31	19.48	4.50	4/21
Stewart, D.E.R.	10	2	181	62	22.62	—					
Stimpson, P.J.	17	1	204	52	12.75	—					
Tolley, C.M.	—	—	—	—	—	—	37	1	—	2.85	1/18
Turner, G.M.	174	10	6144	147	37.46	4	148	7	21.14	4.69	2/25
Warner, A.E.	15	4	45	14	4.09	—	604	19	31.78	4.63	3/26
Watkins, S.G.	1	0	24	24	—	—					
Watson, G.G.	1	0	2	2	—	—	66	7	9.43	4.77	4/30
Webster, A.J.	4	3	13	9*	13.00	—	213	5	42.60	4.44	2/26
Weston, M.J.	91	14	1603	107	20.81	1	1694	57	29.71	4.37	4/11
Wilcock, H.G.	40	15	317	43*	12.68	—					
Wilkinson, K.W.	20	5	221	60	14.73	—	299	4	74.75	5.16	2/29
Yardley, T.J.	70	12	1090	64	18.79	—	3	0	—	3.00	
Younis Ahmed	55	7	1737	113	36.18	2	579	13	44.53	4.91	3/26

3

Club Records

Batting

Double Centuries

405* G.A. Hick v Som., Taunton 1988
311* G.M. Turner v. War., Worcester 1982
276 F.L. Bowley v Hants, Dudley 1914
262* M. Nichol v Hants, Bournemouth 1930
259 D. Kenyon v Yorks., Kidderminster 1956
253* D. Kenyon v Leics., Worcester 1954
246* R.E. Foster v Kent, Worcester 1905
239* G.M. Turner v Oxford U, Oxford 1982
238* D. Kenyon v Yorks., Worcester 1953
233 M.J. Horton v Som., Worcester 1962
231* Nawab of Pataudi v Essex, Worcester 1933
229 D. Kenyon v Hants, Portsmouth 1959
228* G.M. Turner v Glos., Worcester 1980
227* G.A. Hick v Notts., Worcester 1986
227 B.L. D'Oliveira v Yorks., Hull 1974
226 C.F. Walters v Kent, Gravesend 1933
224* Nawab of Pataudi v Kent, Worcester 1933
222 Nawab of Pataudi v Som., Weston 1933
221* Younis Ahmed v Notts., Trent Bridge 1979
219* G.A. Hick v Glam., Neath 1986
217 F.L. Bowley v Leics., Stourbridge 1905
216* E. Cooper v War., Dudley 1939
216 H.K. Foster v Som., Worcester 1903
215* L. Outschoorn v Northants, Worcester 1949
215 H.K. Foster v War., Worcester 1908
215 E.G. Arnold v Oxford U, Oxford 1910
214* Nawab of Pataudi v Glam., Worcester 1934
214* G.M. Turner v Oxford U, Worcester 1975
212* H.H.I.H. Gibbons v Northants, Dudley 1939
212 M.J. Horton v Essex, Leyton 1959
212 G.A. Hick v Lancs., Old Trafford 1988
204* J.A. Ormrod v Kent, Dartford 1973
202* D. Kenyon v Hants, Portsmouth 1954
202* G.M. Turner v Cambridge U, Cambridge 1974
202* G.M. Turner v War., Edgbaston 1978
201 F.L. Bowley v Glos., Worcester 1913
201 D. Kenyon v Glam., Stourbridge 1960
200* E.G. Arnold v War., Edgbaston 1909
200* H.H.I.H. Gibbons v West Indies, Worcester 1928
200* L. Outschoorn v Scotland, Dundee 1951
200* D. Kenyon v Notts. Worcester 1957
200* J.A. Ormrod v Glos., Worcester 1982

Record Wicket Partnerships

1st wicket
309   H.K. Foster & F.L. Bowley v Derby., Derby 1901
306   F.L. Bowley & F.A. Pearson v Glos., Worcester 1913
291   G.M. Turner & J.A. Ormrod v War., Worcester 1982
290   D. Kenyon & P.E. Richardson v Glos., Dudley 1953
279   C.F. Walters & H.H.I.H. Gibbons v Essex, Chelmsford 1934
278* C.F. Walters & H.H.I.H. Gibbons v Leics., Worcester 1934
277   .D. Kenyon & L. Outschoorn v Kent, Gravesend 1954
274   H.K. Foster & F.L. Bowley v Hants, Portsmouth 1907
259   R.G.A. Headley & G.M. Turner v War., Worcester 1972
254   G.M. Turner & J.A. Ormrod v Surrey, Worcester 1978

2nd wicket
287* T.S. Curtis & G.A. Hick v Glam., Neath 1986
284   T.S. Curtis & G.A. Hick v West Indies, Worcester 1988
276   T.S. Curtis & G.A. Hick v Hants, Worcester 1988
274   H.H.I.H. Gibbons & Nawab of Pataudi v Kent, Worcester 1933
258   T.S. Curtis & G.A. Hick v Middx., Lord's 1987
250   F.L. Bowley & H.K. Foster v Som., Worcester 1903

3rd wicket
314   M.J. Horton & T.W. Graveney v Som., Worcester 1962
306   L.G. Crawley & W.V. Fox v Northants, Worcester 1923
303   H.K. Foster & R.E. Foster v Kent, Worcester 1907
279   H.H.I.H. Gibbons & S.H. Martin v Northants, Stourbridge 1934
278   J.A. Ormrod & Imran Khan v War., Worcester 1976
277* G.R. Cass & T.J. Yardley v Leics., Leicester 1975
266   J.D. Inchmore & J.M. Parker v Essex, Worcester 1974
250   C.H. Bull & H.H.I.H. Gibbons v Northants, Kidderminster 1937

4th wicket
281   J.A. Ormrod & Younis Ahmed v Notts., Trent Bridge 1979
277   H.H.I.H. Gibbons & B.W. Quaife v Middx., Worcester 1931
271   T.W. Graveney & B.L. D'Oliveira v Essex, Worcester 1966
260   C.F. Walters & C.H. Bull v Kent, Gravesend 1933
256   C.F. Walters & M. Nichol v Hants, Bournemouth 1933
254   F. Chester & G.N. Foster v Middx., Lord's 1913
250   H.H.I.H. Gibbons & M. Nichol v War., Dudley 1929

5th wicket
393   E.G. Arnold & W.B. Burns v War., Edgbaston 1909
261   H.H.I.H. Gibbons & C.H. Palmer v Northants, Dudley 1939
227   T.S. Curtis & M.J. Weston v Surrey, Worcester 1985
207* H.H.I.H. Gibbons & S.H. Martin v Hants, Worcester 1939
203   M.J. Horton & G. Dews v Essex, Leyton 1959

6th wicket
265   G.A. Hick & S.J. Rhodes v Som., Taunton 1988
227   E.J.O. Hemsley & D.N. Patel v Oxford U, Oxford 1976
206   P.A. Neale & S.J. Rhodes v Derby., Derby 1988
195   G.N. Foster & J.A. Cuffe v Leics., Worcester 1913

7th wicket
205   G.A. Hick & P.J. Newport v Yorks., Worcester 1988
197   H.H.I.H. Gibbons & R. Howorth v Surrey, The Oval 1938
190   R.E.S. Wyatt & R.O. Jenkins v Leics., Worcester 1949
181   G.N. Foster & W.B. Burns v Hants, Worcester 1905
156   D.W. Richardson & N. Gifford v Surrey, The Oval 1961

8th wicket
177*   G.A. Hick & R.K. Illingworth v Som., Taunton 1988
145*   F. Chester & W.H. Taylor v Essex, Worcester 1914
133*   P.A. Neale & G.A. Hick v Surrey, The Oval

9th wicket
181   J.A. Cuffe & R.D. Burrows v Glos., Worcester 1907
141   W.V. Fox & C.V. Tarbox v War., Edgbaston 1929
127   Imran Khan & N. Gifford v Northants, Northampton 1976
113   R.K. Illingworth & N.V. Radford v Notts., Trent Bridge 1988
109   S.J. Rhodes & R.K. Illingworth v Surrey, Worcester 1989

10th wicket
119   W.B. Burns & G.A. Wilson v Som., Worcester 1906
 97   A. Bird & G.A. Wilson v London County, Worcester 1900
 94   R.D. Burrows & E.W. Bale v Yorks., Worcester 1910
 93   C.F. Root & R.T.D. Perks v Derby., Kidderminster 1930

Carrying Bat throughout a Completed Innings

Player	Score	Innings Score	Opponent	Location	Year
F.L. Bowley	104*	207	Middx.	Lord's	1911
F.A. Pearson	154*	342	Surrey	Dudley	1912
F.A. Pearson	67*	152	Sussex	Eastbourne	1914
F.A. Pearson	151*	275	War.	Worcester	1921
F.A. Pearson	68*	123	Hants	Southampton	1923
B.W. Quaife	31*	112	Kent	Stourbridge	1931
H.H.I.H. Gibbons	70*	165	War.	Kidderminster	1934
C.H. Bull	57*	150	Lancs.	Kidderminster	1935 (1st inns)
H.H.I.H. Gibbons	82*	148	Lancs.	Kidderminster	1935 (2nd inns)
F.B. Warne	43*	153	Middx.	Lord's	1937
E. Cooper	104*	273	Lancs.	Old Trafford	1939
E. Cooper	69*	154	War.	Dudley	1951
P.E. Richardson	91*	155	Hants	Worcester	1955
D. Kenyon	103*	215	Hants	Bournemouth	1955
M.J. Horton	53*	91	Lancs.	Old Trafford	1966
G.M. Turner	88*	202	Som.	Worcester	1972
J.A. Ormrod	66*	187	Essex	Chelmsford	1975
J.A. Ormrod	36*	73	Sussex	Worcester	1977
G.M. Turner	141*	169	Glam.	Swansea	1977
J.A. Ormrod	126*	219	Hants	Bournemouth	1980
J.A. Ormrod	63*	136	Derby.	Derby	1983

Century on First-Class Debut for the County

Player	Score	Opponent	Location	Year
M. Nichol	104	West Indies	Worcester	1928
C.A.F. Fiddian-Green	108	Essex	Worcester	1931
D.A. Banks	100	Oxford U	Oxford	1983
C.L. King	123	Som.	Worcester	1983

NB   Fiddian-Green and King had both played first-class cricket for other teams.

Century Before Lunch by One Batsman

Player	Score	Lunch Score	Opponents	Location	Day	Season
R.E. Foster	136	107*	Glos.	Worcester	second	1901
R.E. Foster	111	111	Derby.	Derby	second	1901
H.K. Foster	112	112	Derby.	Worcester	third	1902
W.B. Burns	165	—	Oxford U	Worcester	first	1904
G.F. Wheldon	103	103	Leics.	Leicester	second	1904
H.K. Foster	180	—	Som.	Worcester	first	1905
R.E. Foster	144	—	Glos.	Worcester	first	1907
F.L. Bowley	106	106	Hants	Southampton	first	1908
G.H.T. Simpson-Hayward	105	105	Oxford U	Oxford	first	1908
F.L. Bowley	157	—	War.	Worcester	first	1910
G.N. Foster	129*	129*	Sussex	Worcester	second	1910
F.A. Pearson	113	100*	Middx.	Worcester	third	1910
H.K. Foster	106	106	Som.	Worcester	third	1911
F.L. Bowley	201	100*	Glos.	Worcester	first	1913
F.L. Bowley	276	—	Hants	Dudley	first	1914
F.L. Bowley	131	125*	Essex	Leyton	first	1920
H.H.I.H. Gibbons	107	107	Hants	Southampton	first	1928
B.P. King	124	—	Hants	Worcester	second	1938
A.P. Singleton	152	—	Hants	Southampton	second	1946
R.G. Broadbent	108	108	Leics.	Leicester	third	1952
P.E. Richardson	116	—	Derby.	Derby	first	1957
G.M. Turner	140	123*	Notts.	Worcester	first	1973
J.M. Parker	140	105*	Essex	Worcester	second	1974
J.M. Parker	133	112*	Notts.	Worcester	second	1975
G.M. Turner	150	109*	Surrey	Worcester	first	1978
P.A. Neale	101*	101*	War.	Worcester	third	1979
(G.M. Turner also scored more than 100 runs in this session)						
G.M. Turner	101	101	War.	Edgbaston	first	1980
G.M. Turner	161	126*	Northants	Stourbridge	first	1981
G.M. Turner	311*	128*	War.	Worcester	first	1982
G.M. Turner	115	115	Lancs.	Worcester	third	1982

Adding 100-Plus Runs Before Lunch, Having Started Innings Previous Day

Player	Final Score	Over-night	Lunch	Opponents	Location	Day	Season
R.E. Foster	246*	47*	181*	Kent	Worcester	third	1905
H.L. Higgins	133	29*	129*	Essex	Leyton	third	1919
H.H.I.H. Gibbons	140	0*	140	Kent	Worcester	third	1928
G. Dews	101*	1*	101*	Hants	Dudley	third	1950
P.E. Richardson	134	12*	122*	Notts.	Worcester	third	1956
G.M. Turner	108	1*	108	War.	Worcester	third	1979
G.M. Turner	228*	20	134*	Glos.	Worcester	third	1980

Fastest Century

R.E. Foster (111) reached 100* in 60 minutes v Derby., Derby 1901

Fastest Double Century

H.K. Foster (216) reached 200* in 150 minutes v Som., Worcester 1903

NB   The fastest innings for Worcestershire was probably played by J.D. Inchmore, whose score of 30 v Glos at Cheltenham in 1973 took him only 5 minutes.

Century in Each Innings of Match

R.E. Foster, 134 & 101 v Hants, Worcester 1899
W.L. Foster, 140 & 172* v Hants, Worcester 1899
   (first instance of two batsmen scoring two separate 100s in same match)
E.G. Arnold, 101* & 128 v Cambridge U, Cambridge 1903
M.K. Foster, 141 & 106 v Hants, Worcester 1926
H.H.I.H. Gibbons, 111* & 100* v Hants, Worcester 1939
E. Cooper, 191 & 106* v Northants, Kidderminster 1946
R.G.A. Headley, 187 & 108 v Northants, Worcester 1971
G.M. Turner, 122 & 128* v War., Edgbaston 1972
J.A. Ormrod, 101 & 131* v Som., Worcester 1980
G.M. Turner, 161 & 101 v Northants, Stourbridge 1981
G.M. Turner, 147* & 139 v War., Worcester 1981

Batsmen Scoring 2000 or more Runs in a Season

H.H.I.H. Gibbons	2654	(52.03)	1934
G.A. Hick	2615	(79.24)	1988
D. Kenyon	2430	(55.22)	1954
G.M. Turner	2379	(61.00)	1970
T.W. Graveney	2375	(55.23)	1964
C.F. Walters	2292	(53.30)	1933
D. Kenyon	2278	(49.52)	1953
D. Kenyon	2174	(45.29)	1950

D. Kenyon	2160	(39.27)	1957
M. Nichol	2154	(43.95)	1933
D. Kenyon	2133	(41.82)	1951
D. Kenyon	2126	(40.88)	1952
M.J. Horton	2123	(44.22)	1959
H.H.I.H. Gibbons	2120	(43.26)	1938
G.M. Turner	2101	(55.28)	1981
P.E. Richardson	2029	(39.01)	1953
R.G.A. Headley	2026	(32.67)	1961
H.H.I.H. Gibbons	2008	(37.88)	1933
G.A. Hick	2004	(64.64)	1986

Bowling

Hat Tricks in First-Class Matches

G.A. Wilson v London County, Worcester 1900
G.A. Wilson v Surrey, Worcester 1901
G.A. Wilson v Australia, Worcester 1905
J.A. Cuffe v Hants, Bournemouth 1910
W.B. Burns v Glos., Worcester 1913
F.A. Pearson v Surrey, Worcester 1914
C.R. Preece v War., Edgbaston 1924
R.T.D. Perks v Kent, Stourbridge 1931
R.T.D. Perks v War., Edgbaston 1933
P.F. Jackson v Glam., Neath 1936
R.O. Jenkins v Surrey, The Oval 1948
R.O. Jenkins v Surrey, Worcester 1949
R.O. Jenkins v Surrey, Worcester 1949
   (in each innings of same match)
R. Howorth v War., Edgbaston 1950
J.A. Flavell v Kent, Kidderminster 1951
J.A. Flavell v Cambridge U, Cambridge 1953
M.J. Horton v Som., Bath 1956
L.J. Coldwell v Leics., Stourbridge 1957
J.A. Flavell v Lancs., Old Trafford 1963
L.J. Coldwell v Essex, Brentwood 1965
R.G.M. Carter v Lancs., Worcester 1965
N. Gifford v Derby., Chesterfield 1965
J. Cumbes v Northants, Worcester 1977
H.L. Alleyne v Middx., Lord's 1981

Nine Wickets in an Innings
(NB   no instance of all 10 wickets has been recorded)

9–23   C.F. Root v Lancs., Worcester 1931

9–30   J.A. Flavell v Kent, Dover 1955
9–38   J.A. Cuffe v Yorks., Bradford 1907
9–38   A.J. Conway v Glos., Moreton-in-Marsh 1914
9–40   C.F. Root v Essex, Worcester 1924
9–40   R.T.D. Perks v Glam., Stourbridge 1939
9–42   R.T.D. Perks v Glos., Cheltenham, 1946
9–45   P.F. Jackson v Som., Dudley 1935
9–56   M.J. Horton v South Africa, Worcester 1955
9–56   J.A. Flavell v Middx., Kidderminster 1964
9-64   E.G. Arnold v Oxford U, Oxford 1905
9–70   N.V. Radford v Som., Worcester 1986
9–75   G.A. Wilson v Oxford U, Oxford 1904
9–81   C.F. Root v Kent, Tunbridge Wells, 1930
9–122 J.A. Flavell v Sussex, Hastings 1954

Fourteen or More Wickets in a Match

15–87   A.J. Conway v Glos., Moreton-in-Marsh 1914
15–106 R.T.D. Perks v Essex, Worcester 1937
15–122 R.O. Jenkins v Sussex, Dudley 1953
15–142 G.A. Wilson v Som., Taunton 1905
14–76   N. Gifford v Cambridge U, Cambridge 1972
14–96   R.T.D. Perks v Glos., Cheltenham 1946
14–107 S.H. Martin v Kent, Gillingham 1939
14–109 A. Bird v Hants, Southampton 1901
14–110 S.H. Martin v Som., Bath 1937
14–115 J.A. Cuffe v Glos., Dudley 1911

125 or More Wickets in a Season

C.F. Root	207	(17.52)	1925
C.F. Root	168	(20.25)	1923
R.O. Jenkins	159	(20.84)	1949
J.A. Flavell	158	(17.21)	1961
R.T.D. Perks	154	(18.83)	1939
C.F. Root	152	(16.01)	1934
C.F. Root	148	(22.06)	1929
C.F. Root	145	(17.91)	1927
J.A. Flavell	142	(14.78)	1965
L.J. Coldwell	140	(19.25)	1961
R.T.D. Perks	139	(20.59)	1937
L.J. Coldwell	139	(17.97)	1962
R. Howorth	138	(16.09)	1947
R.O. Jenkins	138	(23.31)	1951
R.T.D. Perks	136	(23.97)	1938
J.A. Flavell	135	(14.00)	1966
R.T.D. Perks	134	(18.44)	1936
N. Gifford	133	(19.66)	1961
G.W. Brook	132	(21.88)	1930
C.F. Root	131	(22.61)	1930
R. Howorth	127	(19.47)	1936
C.F. Root	126	(16.03)	1931

R.T.D. Perks	126	(22.04)	1935
J.A. Flavell	126	(20.06)	1960
E.G. Arnold	125	(17.19)	1903
R. Howorth	125	(19.61)	1935

All-round Records

100 Runs and 10 Wickets in One Match

E.G. Arnold	200*	3–70	7–44	v War.	Edgbaston	1909
Imran Khan	111*	7–53	6–46	v Lancs.	Worcester	1976

1000 Runs and 100 Wickets in One Season

Player	Runs	Average	Wickets	Average	Year
E.G. Arnold	1040	(31.51)	125	(17.19)	1903
J.A. Cuffe	1054	(25.70)	110	(23.56)	1911
F.A. Pearson	1052	(25.04)	111	(22.89)	1923
C.F. Root	1044	(20.88)	118	(29.26)	1928
S.H. Martin	1130	(21.73)	114	(20.25)	1937
R. Howorth	1019	(21.22)	100	(24.34)	1939
S.H. Martin	1262	(25.24)	106	(25.00)	1939
R. Howorth	1050	(22.82)	104	(20.18)	1946
R. Howorth	1172	(24.93)	138	(16.09)	1947
M.J. Horton	1808	(29.16)	101	(21.12)	1961

Wicketkeeping

Six or More Dismissals in One Innings

Total	ct	st	Player	Opponent	Location	Year
7	1	6	H. Yarnold	Scotland	Broughty Ferry	1951
6	4	2	G.W. Gaukrodger	Kent	Tunbridge Wells	1907
6	2	4	E.W. Bale	Australians	Worcester	1909
6	3	3	H. Yarnold	Hants	Worcester	1949
6	6	0	G.R. Cass	Essex	Worcester	1973
6	6	0	H.G. Wilcock	Hants	Portsmouth	1974
6	6	0	S.J. Rhodes	Sussex	Kidderminster	1988
6	6	0	S.J. Rhodes	War.,	Edgbaston	1989

Eight or More Dismissals in One Match

Total	ct	st	Player	Opponent	Location	Year
9	5	4	H. Yarnold	Hants	Worcester	1949
9	9	0	S.J. Rhodes	Sussex	Kidderminster	1988
8	7	1	E.W. Bale	Glos.	Cheltenham	1913
8	4	4	H. Yarnold	Kent	Dover	1949
8	3	5	H. Yarnold	Cambridge U	Worcester	1950
8	1	7	H. Yarnold	Scotland	Broughty Ferry	1951
8	8	0	R. Booth	Essex	Romford	1962
8	7	1	D.J. Humphries	Derby.	Derby	1979

Seventy or More Dismissals in One Season

Total	ct	st	Player	Year
104	59	45	H. Yarnold	1949
101	85	16	R. Booth	1960
100	90	10	R. Booth	1964
97	83	14	R. Booth	1962
95	59	36	H. Yarnold	1951
94	62	32	H. Yarnold	1950
90	74	16	R. Booth	1961
88	83	5	R. Booth	1959
78	70	8	S.J. Rhodes	1988
78	59	19	R. Booth	1957
72	64	8	R. Booth	1966

300 and More Dismissals in Career

Total	ct	st	Player	Year
1015	868	147	R. Booth	1956–70
684	458	226	H. Yarnold	1938–55
345	286	59	D.J. Humphries	1977–85
324	293	31	S.J. Rhodes	1985–date
319	234	85	E.W. Bale	1908–20

Five Catches in One Innings

6 R.G. Broadbent v Glam., Stourbridge 1960
5 G.N. Foster v Hants, Southampton 1911
5 L. Outschoorn v Derbys., Kidderminster 1948
5 R.G.A. Headley v Kent, Dartford 1964
5 R.G.A. Headley v Glos., Cheltenham 1967
5 G.A. Hick v Lancs., Old Trafford 1989

Seven Catches in One Match

8 W.B. Burns v Yorks., Bradford 1907
7 R.G. Broadbent v Glamorgan, Stourbridge 1960

Forty or More Catches in One Season

65	D.W. Richardson	1961
55	L. Outschoorn	1959
51	D.W. Richardson	1964
49	R.G.A. Headley	1964
43	L. Outschoorn	1951
42	D.W. Richardson	1962
41	D.W. Richardson	1963

250 or More Catches in a Career

414	D.W. Richardson	1952–67
384	J.A. Ormrod	1962–83
353	G. Dews	1946–61
343	R.G.A. Headley	1958–74
306	D. Kenyon	1946–67
297	R.G. Broadbent	1950–63
276	L. Outschoorn	1946–59
259	Norman Gifford	1960–82

Afterword

by Roly Jenkins

This afterword has three distinct ingredients: pleasure, nostalgia and sadness.

Pleasure indeed for the privilege to comment on the cricket scene in a 'then and now' vein. Years ago (at least ten), two former captains of Worcestershire CCC, namely C.F. Walters and the late Lord Cobham, both remarked to me that they felt lucky to have played first-class cricket at the right time and the best, implying that they were not too happy with the first-class cricket scene at the time of comment. I shudder to think what their thoughts would be at the state of the game today.

I joined Worcestershire as a colt in 1936 and stayed with the club until 1958, making a lot of friends but not much money – though friendship cannot be measured in financial terms. My time encompassed a period when the game had many outstanding characters: there are too many to mention, but my personal idol was Denis Compton, a great batsman, a cricketer's man and extrovert extraordinaire. In my time, there was great camaraderie between the players of opposing teams; this is not so evident these days where money, and not the game, is the motivation.

The nostalgia, of course, lies in the many funny incidents that occurred during my playing days on and off the field – so many in fact that they would occupy a good deal of this book. Yes, I do indeed count myself fortunate to have played with a lot of delightful people – ordinary, like yours truly, and many extraordinary.

Unfortunately, I now come to the sad part of this afterword: the near extinction of the spin bowlers and the exploitation of the bouncers and seam bowlers. Today, the condition of wickets, the lush grass of the outfields, the laws of the game and even the cricket ball itself, all lend themselves to placing a premium on the fast and seam bowlers. A shiny new ball is a weapon in the hands of the pace-men. The spinner is not allowed to interfere with the ball, except to shine it, which is no advantage to him. These days, in my opinion, the pace-men get their wickets far too easily. If four-day games are to be the vogue then four-day wickets should be provided. The preponderance of bouncers and short-pitched deliveries has robbed the game of the spin bowler's artistry.

I would like to see two laws brought in for the betterment of the game. First, any ball bouncing above normal shoulder height should be pronounced a 'dead ball' and four runs conceded, thereby eliminating the use of helmets for batsmen. Secondly, no fielder should be allowed within five to six yards in front of the wicket; then they would not require helmets or protective clothing. Would you, dear reader, go to the cinema or theatre if you were unable to see the performers' faces?

I do not look back at my youth through rose-tinted glasses and think that we were better players in my day than now. Comparisons are indeed odious! However, I think we were more entertaining, and cricket was more about fun and not battles. Yes, I probably played cricket at the right and best time …

I trust this book, with its many statistics, will give pleasure to its readers. However, do remember that cricketing greatness does not reside in figures but in good sporting behaviour and humility.

Subscribers

Robert Brooke
David Goodyear
Roly Jenkins
Revd Mike Vockins
T. Airey
E.J. Allaway
A.T. Amos
John L. Anderton
Trevor Auty
Stephen Bagust
R. Baker
Richard S. Baker
G.W. Barker
Peter Barnsley
W. Baylis
Gordon Bearne
J.C. Bell
David John Bennett
Kevin J. Billingham
Tony Blake
Margaret Bolton
Paul Bolton
Paul Bonas
T.M.T. Bruce-Morgan
S.J. Brueton
J.R. Bullock
P.N. Burley
D.H. Burt
D.J. and C. Bust
E.N. Campbell
John Carter
Frances Cartwright
Rebecca J. Cartwright
Simon J. Cartwright
G. Colley
Andy Colquhoun
Leslie Cook
Gary James Cowley
John Crofts
D.J. Derricott
W.R. Edwards
C.H. Emms
Peter Evans

T.G. Evans
Neil Featonby
Geoffrey John Field
Peter Flynn
Anthony O. Fowler
J. Francis
Andrew Frisby
P.N. Gammon
A.A.B. Gilburt
Simon D. Goodyear
William V. Goodyear
M.F. Green
James C. Greenway
M.G.G. Gregory
John Griffiths
Roger Groves
Lionel Guest
Maria Hanks
A.J. Harley
Robert Harley
Brian T. Harris
Peter Daniel Harris
P.R. Harris
I.M. Harrison
The Revd J.B. Harrop
Les Hatton
Bernard Herring
Olive Higgins
P.G. Higgins
Mom, Dad, Lesley and family
(Hill)
P.N. Hines
M.J. Holmes
Neil Homer
Martin Horton
David and Sue Huband
John and Sally Huband
N.H. Humphries
Ray Hunt
Paul K. Jacobs
S. Jacques
N.D.L.L. James
B.E. Jenkins
Andrew David Johnson

R.J. Johnson
C. Lloyd Jones
Gordon Jones
Tim Jones
F.G.W. Keep
Jim Lacey
A.A. Lamb
R.H. Lander
Freddie Lloyd
Paul Lockley
Andrew Lowe
Alastair Mackinnon
Colin Mann
Tim Mann
H.G. Martin
P.F. Michael
John Millward
Roger J. Mills
Ray Moore
U.A. Mullen
F.W. Needham
Frank W. Noble
Dennis A. Paine
David J. Parkes
Frank Pattison
Ken Pattison
J.R. Peace
G.H. Perkins
P.J. Perry
M.A. Peter
G. Donald Pickering
Anthony William Price
David Pryke
John Pugh
Dr P.S. Raderecht
G. Rathbone
John Reeves
Trevor J. Reynolds
D.J. Richards
J.E. Richards
J.T. Rickards
W.J. Ricketts
B.S. Roberts
Timothy Roberts

M.A. Rogers
David Rose
J.M. Round
D.P. Rowlands
E.H. Ruston
Ben Schiffmann
Fiona C. Scott
J.E. Scott
A. Scrafton
G.D. Scrafton
R.B. Screen
G.H. Sharp
Dawson Simpson
Paul Skett
P. Skidmore
A.G. Smith
M. Smith
R.W. Smith
Stephen J. Smith
M. Southall
Brian Spawton
P.E. Spear
Michael W. Stanley
Peter J. Stanley
Dave Stephens
R. Tedstone
James J. Tibbets
R.L. Tolley
J. Townsend
M.E. Townsend
Colin J. Tudge
Mike Vass
John C. Vine
T.P. Walker
John Walls
David Wareing
John Waters
A.P. Weston
J.C. Weston
P.G. Westwood
Patrick J. Whitehead
Brian Lance Whitehouse
Peter Willis
I.R.H. Winnard
W.G. Woodcock